101 Things®

To Do With

an

Air Fryer

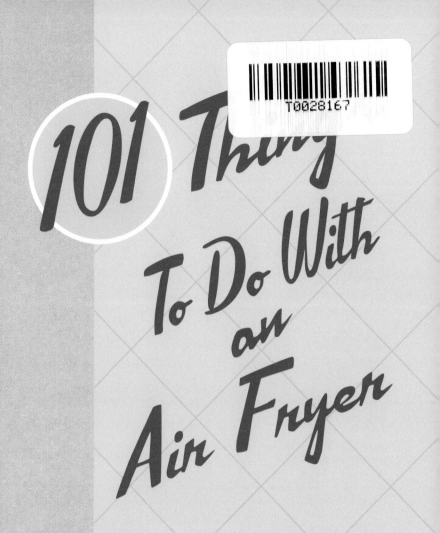

101 Things To Do With an Air Fryer

BY DONNA KELLY

GIBBS SMITH
TO ENRICH AND INSPIRE HUMANKIND

First Edition
25 24 23 22   5 4 3 2

Published by
Gibbs Smith
P.O. Box 667
Layton, Utah 84041

1.800.835.4993 orders
www.gibbs-smith.com

Designed by Renee Bond
Printed and bound in Korea
Gibbs Smith books are printed on either recycled, 100% post-consumer
waste, FSC-certified papers or on paper produced from sustainable PEFC-
certified forest/controlled wood source. Learn more at www.pefc.org.

Library of Congress Cataloging-in-Publication Data
Names: Kelly, Donna, 1955- author.
Identifiers: LCCN 2020033168 | ISBN 9781423657224
(spiral bound) | ISBN 9781423657231 (epub)
Subjects: LCSH: Hot air frying. | LCGFT: Cookbooks.
Classification: LCC TX689 .K45 2021 | DDC 641.7/7--dc23
LC record available at https://lccn.loc.gov/2020033168
ISBN: 978-1-4236-5722-4

Dedicated to all passionate home cooks who delight in making healthy yet delicious food.

CONTENTS

Helpful Hints 9

Bountiful Breakfasts

Let's Do Lunch

Appetizers & Snacks

Sumptuous Sides

Beef & Pork Main Dishes

Quick Carne Asada 62 • Shepherd's Pie Twice-Baked Potatoes 63 • Chimichurri Skirt Steak 64 • Tuesday Night Beef Bulgogi 65 • Pizza Supreme-Stuffed Peppers 66 • Shortcut Calzones 67 • Miso and Honey-Glazed Pork Chops 68 • Italian Mini Meatloaves 69 • Marinated Pork Tenderloin 70 • Balsamic Steak and Veggie Bundles 71 • Italian Zucchini Spirals 72

Poultry Main Dishes

Crispy Skin Turkey Breast 74 • Pickle-Brined Air-Fried Chicken 75 • Santa Fe Chicken Casserole 76 • 3 Ms Chicken Thighs 77 • Creamy Tinga Taquitos 78 • Chicken Satay Skewers with Peanut Sauce 79 • Ritzy Chicken Tenders 80 • Inside-Out Chicken Cordon Bleu 81 • Tandoori Chicken Thighs 82 • Lasagna-Stuffed Chicken Breasts 83 • Hot-Honey Chicken 84 • Weeknight Chicken Adobo 85

Seafood Main Dishes

Sheet Pan Shrimp Boil 88 • Coconut, Cashew, and Curry Cod 89 • Salmon Croquettes 90 • Heavenly Halibut 91 • Grownup Fish Sticks 92 • Old Bay Shrimp, Tomatoes, and Feta 93 • Asian-Glazed Salmon 94 • Coconut Bang Bang Shrimp 95

Vegetarian Main Dishes

Caprese Stuffed Portobellos 98 • Greek Zucchini-Feta Casserole 99 • Pizza-Topped Frittata 100 • Four Cheese Zucchini Cakes 101 • Phyllo-Topped Spinach Pie 102 • General Tso's Cauliflower 103 • Buttermilk Air-Fried Mushrooms 104 • Zucchini Burrito Boats 105 • Twice-Baked Butternut Squash 106 • Thai Sesame-Crusted Tofu 107 • Air-Fryer Eggplant Pizzas 108

Sweet Treats

Triple Berry Crisp 110 • Pink Pears in Puff Pastry 111 • Spice Cake in Baked Apple Shells 112 • Campfire-Free S'mores Dessert 113 • Apple-Cinnamon Chips with Almond Dip 114 • Flourless Brownie Cookies 115 • Shortcut Apple Crostata 116 • Berries and Cream Dessert Nachos 117 • Best-Ever Chocolate Chip Cookies 118 • Four-Ingredient Shortbread Cookies 119 • Apple Pie Egg Rolls 120 • Fruit-Topped Cheesecake Tart 121 • State Fair-Style Funnel Cakes 122 • Summer Fruit Shortcakes 123 • Air-Fryer Banana Boats 124

HELPFUL HINTS

1. Congratulations on your use of one of the most innovative products for busy home cooks: the air fryer! This appliance will revolutionize the way you cook. Air fryers cook food very quickly and your food will be crispy on the outside without a ton of oil that is needed with the use of a deep fryer.

2. These recipes were created with a toaster oven–style air fryer, which came with a rack, a wire basket, and a baking sheet. Most recipes use either the wire basket or the baking sheet. If your air fryer does not have a baking sheet, use aluminum foil to line the air fryer basket whenever the recipe calls for use of a baking sheet.

3. Please note that food should be cooked in batches as needed to fit your air fryer.

4. Make adjustments to the recipe volume to fit the capacity of your air fryer.

5. Most recipes call for use of cooking oil spray, which is not listed as an ingredient because it is used mostly for spraying pans or spraying food before air frying.

6. Cooking oil spray is also a great replacement for brushing oil on food because very little oil is needed to coat the food before cooking.

7. Most air fryers don't require preheating. Consult the manufacturer's recommendations for your equipment. If you find that you prefer crispier food, try preheating your air fryer at the temperature needed for the recipe for 7 minutes prior to baking.

8. Some recipes in this cookbook provide preheating instructions as needed for the specific dish being made.

BOUNTIFUL BREAKFASTS

BREAKFAST SCRAMBLE QUESADILLAS

1/2 cup	**diced ham, bacon, or sausage**
6	**large eggs**
2 tablespoons	**milk**
1/2 teaspoon each	**salt and pepper**
1/2 cup	**thinly sliced green onions**
8 (6-inch)	**thin flour tortillas**
4 tablespoons	**cream cheese,** softened
1 cup	**grated cheddar cheese**
1/2 cup	**grated pepper jack cheese**
	salsa, for serving

Spray a medium skillet with cooking oil and saute ham over medium-high heat for about 2 minutes, until lightly browned. Whisk together eggs, milk, salt, and pepper. Pour into skillet, stir, and cook until scrambled but still moist. Turn off heat and stir in green onions.

Lay 1 tortilla on a cutting board. Spread 1 tablespoon cream cheese on tortilla. Spread 1/2 cup of scrambled mixture evenly over tortilla. Sprinkle 1/4 cup cheddar and 2 tablespoons pepper jack cheese over top of scrambled mixture. Place another tortilla on top and press down with a large spatula.

Place on baking sheet and bake in air fryer at 325 degrees F for 3 minutes. Turn quesadilla over and cook another 2 minutes. Repeat steps with remaining ingredients. Serve immediately with salsa. Makes 4 quesadillas.

SHEET PAN BREAKFAST HASH

1	**large russet potato**
1 (1/2-inch-thick)	**slice ham**
1/2	**green bell pepper,** chopped
1/2	**onion,** chopped
	salt and pepper, to taste
1/2 cup	**grated cheddar cheese**
4	**large eggs**

Cut potato in half lengthwise. Spray cut sides with a little cooking oil and place cut side down on baking sheet. Bake in air fryer at 375 degrees F for 30 minutes. Remove potato and let cool to warm. Peel potato halves and then dice into 1/2-inch cubes.

Spray baking sheet with oil. Cut ham into 1/2-inch cubes. Scatter potato, bell pepper, onion, and ham on baking sheet. Sprinkle with salt and pepper. Spray with oil. Bake in air fryer at 450 degrees F for 3 minutes. Stir and bake for another 2 minutes.

Sprinkle cheese on top and then make 4 indentations in mixture with a large spoon, about 3-inch circles. Crack 1 egg in each indentation. Bake in air fryer at 300 degrees for a few minutes, until eggs are cooked to desired doneness, about 3 minutes for runny yolks. Sprinkle with salt and pepper and serve immediately. Makes 4 servings.

STUFFED BREAKFAST BUNDLES

1 tablespoon	**butter**
6	**large eggs**
2 tablespoons	**milk**
$^1/_4$ cup	**diced red bell pepper**
$^1/_4$ cup	**diced cooked bacon**
1 package (16 ounces)	**uncooked refrigerated biscuits** (8 count)
1 cup	**grated cheddar cheese**

In a medium skillet, melt butter over medium heat. Whisk eggs and milk and pour into skillet. Stir and cook until eggs are almost set. Turn off heat. Stir in bell pepper and bacon.

Separate biscuits and roll each biscuit out to a 6-inch circle. Scatter a little cheese on each circle. Place $^1/_4$ cup of egg mixture in center of each circle of dough. Bring up opposite sides of circle up over top of egg mixture. Pinch dough together. Bring up the opposite ends of circle, evenly spaced out, to meet the pinched dough over the top of the egg mixture. Pinch together at top. Repeat with remaining circles and egg mixture.

Place stuffed bundles on baking sheet, spaced apart. Bake in air fryer at 325 degrees F for 8 minutes. Serve immediately. Makes 8 bundles.

MINI BREAKFAST CASSEROLES

2 tablespoons	**butter,** melted
1 cup	**frozen hash brown potatoes**
6	**large eggs**
2 tablespoons	**milk**
1/2 cup	**diced red bell pepper**
3	**green onions,** thinly sliced
1 cup	**grated Monterey Jack cheese**
1/2 teaspoon each	**salt and pepper**
1/2 cup	**grated cheddar cheese**

Preheat a 6-cup jumbo muffin tin or 6 (1-cup) ramekins in air fryer at 350 degrees F for 5 minutes. Pour 1 teaspoon melted butter into each of the muffin cups or ramekins, swirling to coat bottoms. Spoon hash browns into each cup and brush with more melted butter. Bake in air fryer for 3 minutes.

Whisk together eggs, milk, bell pepper, green onions, Monterey Jack cheese, salt, and pepper. Evenly divide mixture into muffin cups. Sprinkle cheddar cheese on top.

Bake in air fryer at 300 degrees F for 8–10 minutes, until lightly browned. Let sit on counter for 5 minutes. Run a knife around edges of muffin cups to release from tin then invert casseroles onto serving plates. Makes 6 servings.

STUFFED FRENCH TOAST ROLLS

6 slices	**firm white bread,** crusts removed
6 tablespoons	**cream cheese,** softened
1 cup	**diced fruit of choice**
3	**large eggs**
1 cup	**milk**
	syrup, for serving

Flatten bread slices lightly with a spatula. Spread cream cheese on 1 side of bread slices. Scatter fruit on top. Roll up each bread slice into a cigar shape.

In a shallow bowl or pan, whisk together eggs and milk. Roll bread rolls in egg mixture. Line air fryer baking sheet with aluminum foil and spray with cooking oil. Place each roll, seam side down, on baking sheet.

Bake in air fryer at 300 degrees F for 8–10 minutes, until lightly browned and cooked through. Serve immediately with syrup. Makes 6 servings.

VARIATION: Chocolate hazelnut spread is a delicious alternative to the cream cheese.

DUTCH BABY PANCAKE

1/2 cup	**flour**
2 tablespoons	**sugar**
1/4 teaspoon	**salt**
3	**large eggs,** at room temperature
2/3 cup	**warm milk**
1 teaspoon	**vanilla extract**
2 tablespoons	**butter**
	syrup or optional topping

Place an 8-inch round cake pan in air fryer and heat at 350 degrees F for 5 minutes.

In a medium bowl, whisk together flour, sugar, and salt. Whisk in eggs then milk and vanilla.

Melt butter in cake pan. Pour in batter. Bake in air fryer for 8 minutes. Serve immediately, drizzled with syrup or with a topping provided below. Makes 4 servings.

OPTIONAL TOPPINGS

Drizzle with warm lemon curd and sprinkle with blueberries and powdered sugar.

Saute thin apple slices in butter and toss with cinnamon and sugar.

Mix cream cheese with a little lemon juice and sugar and drizzle on top. Sprinkle with diced fresh fruit.

ALMOND-COCONUT GRANOLA

I cup	**rolled oats**
1/3 cup	**sliced almonds**
1/3 cup	**unsweetened coconut flakes**
1/3 cup	**sweetened dried cranberries**
1/4 teaspoon	**salt**
3 tablespoons	**melted coconut oil**
1/3 cup	**maple syrup or agave nectar**
1/4 cup	**creamy almond butter**
I teaspoon	**almond extract**
1/2 cup	**chocolate chips,** optional

In a large mixing bowl, stir together oats, almonds, coconut flakes, and cranberries.

Place salt, coconut oil, syrup, almond butter, and almond extract in a small glass bowl. Microwave mixture for about 60 seconds and stir until combined. Toss this mixture with oat mixture in mixing bowl.

Spray baking sheet with cooking oil. Spread mixture on baking sheet. Bake in air fryer at 350 degrees F for 10 minutes, stirring every 3 minutes. Let granola cool and then stir in chocolate chips, if using. Makes 2 cups.

CRUNCHY FRENCH TOAST STICKS

2	**large eggs**
4 tablespoons	**sour cream,** divided
$^1/_2$ cup	**milk**
3 tablespoons	**sugar**
$^1/_2$ teaspoon	**cinnamon**
1 teaspoon	**vanilla extract**
	pinch of salt
6 (1-inch-thick) slices	**stale firm white bread**
1 cup	**cornflake crumbs***
$^1/_2$ cup	**maple syrup**

In a shallow bowl, mix eggs, 3 tablespoons sour cream, milk, sugar, cinnamon, vanilla, and salt. Cut each bread slice into 3 pieces. Place bread sticks in egg mixture. Let sit for 30 seconds or so, turning once. Press all sides of soaked bread sticks in cornflakes.

Spray wire basket with cooking oil. Place bread sticks in basket. Spray with oil. Bake in air fryer at 350 degrees F for 5 minutes. Turn sticks over and spray with oil. Cook another 4–5 minutes, until browned.

Mix together remaining sour cream and maple syrup. Heat in microwave oven for about 20 seconds, until hot. Serve as a dipping sauce for sticks. Makes 4–6 servings.

* You can often purchase cornflake crumbs at the store, but if you cannot find crumbs, use cornflakes. Place cornflakes in a food processor and process until very fine crumbs.

JAM-FILLED POP TARTS

I package (14 ounces)	**refrigerated pie dough** (2 pie circles that are 12 inches in diameter)
6 tablespoons	**fruit-only jam of choice**
$1/2$ cup	**powdered sugar**
2 teaspoons	**lemon juice**
	pinch of salt

Preheat baking sheet in air fryer at 350 degrees F while making pop tarts.

Unroll pie dough circles on a flat surface. Cut into 12 (3 x 4-inch) rectangles. Place 3 rectangles on a piece of aluminum foil that is the size of baking sheet. Place 1 tablespoon of jam in center of each and smooth out a bit, leaving a 1-inch border empty. Spread a little water with your finger around the edges of each of the 3 rectangles. Place 1 of the remaining rectangles on top of each jam-coated rectangle. Crimp edges of each tart with a fork.

Place tarts with foil on top of heated baking sheet. Bake in air fryer at 300 degrees F for 6–8 minutes, until dough is cooked through and lightly browned. Turn off air fryer and let pop tarts sit in air fryer for about 5 minutes, allowing bottoms of pop tarts to finish cooking.

Repeat this process to make remaining 3 pop tarts.

Mix together the powdered sugar, lemon juice, and salt. When pop tarts are cooled to warm, drizzle tops with powdered sugar mixture. Serve immediately. Makes 6 pop tarts.

FAMILY FAVORITE CINNAMON ROLLS

16 ounces	**purchased pizza dough**
6 tablespoons	**butter,** at room temperature, divided
$1/4$ cup	**brown sugar**
1 tablespoon	**cinnamon**
4 ounces	**cream cheese,** softened
1 cup	**powdered sugar**

Let pizza dough come to room temperature on countertop, about 10 minutes. On a lightly floured surface, roll out dough to a 12 x 16-inch rectangle, with widest edge facing you. Spread 4 tablespoons butter on top of dough. Sprinkle brown sugar and cinnamon on top. Roll up, starting with long edge closest to you, to form a 16-inch-long cylinder. Cut into 8 pieces.

Place rolls, spiral side down, on baking sheet. Cover with a kitchen towel and let rise in a warm place for about hour, until double in size.

Bake in air fryer at 325 degrees F for 5 minutes. Turn rolls over and bake another 3 minutes. Meanwhile, stir together the remaining butter, cream cheese, and powdered sugar. Spread on tops of warm rolls. Serve immediately. Makes 8 rolls.

LET'S DO
LUNCH

SONORAN-STYLE HOT DOGS

6 slices	**regular bacon,** not thick cut
6	**hot dogs**
6	**hot dog buns**
	ketchup and mustard, as desired
1 cup	**cooked whole pinto beans**
3/4 cup	**pico de gallo or salsa**

Place bacon slices in a single layer on baking sheet and bake in air fryer at 400 degrees F for about 2 minutes, until softened and slightly cooked but not crispy. Remove bacon from baking sheet and blot with paper towel. Wipe baking sheet off with paper towel.

Wrap 1 slice of bacon around each hot dog, covering entire hot dog and not overlapping. Place covered hot dogs, spaced apart and seam side down, on baking sheet. Bake for 6–8 minutes, until bacon is crispy.

Drizzle insides of hot dog buns with ketchup and mustard as desired. Place 1 hot dog in each bun. Mash pinto beans lightly with a fork and scatter on hot dogs. Sprinkle pico de gallo or salsa on top. Serve immediately. Makes 6 servings.

THREE CHEESE GREEN QUESADILLA

4 tablespoons	**cream cheese,** softened
8 (6-inch)	**flour tortillas**
2 cups	**grated cheddar cheese**
2 cups	**grated Monterey Jack cheese**
2	**green onions,** thinly sliced
I can (4 ounces)	**diced green chiles**
	green salsa, for serving

Spread $^1/_2$ tablespoon cream cheese on 2 tortillas. Sprinkle $^1/_2$ cup cheddar cheese, $^1/_2$ cup Monterey Jack cheese, some green onions, and I tablespoon green chiles on I of the tortillas. Put other tortilla, cream cheese side down, on top, pressing down to adhere together.

Place on baking sheet and bake in air fryer at 375 degrees F for 3 minutes or until top tortilla is golden brown. Turn quesadilla over and bake for another 2 minutes, or until golden brown. Repeat process with remaining ingredients.

Serve immediately with salsa as a garnish. Makes 4 servings.

10 MINUTE TUNA MELTS

3	**English muffins,** split in half
I can (5 ounces)	**tuna in water,** well drained
2 tablespoons	**cream cheese,** softened
2 tablespoons	**minced dill pickle**
4 tablespoons	**finely grated Parmesan cheese,** divided

Set air fryer to toast setting, or to 350 degrees F if there is no toast setting. Toast English muffins for a few minutes until lightly browned.

Mix together tuna, cream cheese, dill pickle, and 2 tablespoons of Parmesan cheese. Spread on toasted muffin halves. Sprinkle remaining Parmesan cheese on tops.

Place topped muffins in air fryer basket and spray with cooking oil. Toast for about 3 minutes, until bubbly and lightly browned. Makes 6 servings.

BLACK BEAN MELTS

2 cans (15 ounces each)	**black beans,** drained and rinsed
1 tablespoon	**ground cumin**
2	**chipotle chiles** (from a small can)*
1 tablespoon	**lime juice**
3	**large hoagie-style sandwich rolls,** cut in half lengthwise
2 tablespoons	**butter,** melted
2 cups	**grated pepper jack cheese**

Place black beans, cumin, chiles, and lime juice in food processor or blender. Blend until very smooth, about 3 minutes, scraping down sides as needed.

Brush cut sides of rolls with butter and place, cut sides up, on air fryer baking sheet. Set air fryer to toast or 350 degrees F and bake rolls until lightly browned, 1–2 minutes.

Spread a thick layer of bean mixture on cut sides of rolls. Spread cheese on top of bean mixture. Bake in air fryer for 3–5 minutes, until cheese is lightly browned and bubbly. Makes 6 servings.

*To decrease the heat level of chipotle peppers, cut them in half and scrape out and discard the seeds.

TURKEY-PARMESAN SLIDERS

I tablespoon	**ketchup**
I teaspoon	**garlic powder**
I teaspoon	**onion powder**
$^1/_4$ cup	**panko-style breadcrumbs**
I	**large egg**
$^1/_2$ teaspoon each	**salt and pepper**
I cup	**finely grated Parmesan cheese,** divided
I6 ounces	**ground turkey**
6	**small buns**
	condiments of choice

Mix together ketchup, garlic powder, onion powder, breadcrumbs, egg, salt, pepper, and $^1/_2$ cup Parmesan cheese. Gently stir in turkey. Using $^1/_3$ cup turkey mixture per patty, form 6 patties about 3 inches in diameter. Refrigerate for I0 minutes.

Spray a baking sheet with cooking oil. Place turkey patties on baking sheet. Spread a thin layer of half of remaining Parmesan cheese on top of each patty, pressing down to adhere cheese to patties. Bake in air fryer at 425 degrees F for 5 minutes.

Turn patties over. Spread a thin layer of remaining Parmesan cheese on top of each patty. Bake in air fryer for another 3 minutes. Serve on buns with condiments as desired. Makes 6 servings.

EASY PEASY PIZZA

2 tablespoons	**cornmeal**
8 ounces	**purchased pizza dough**
2 tablespoons	**olive oil**
$^1/_2$ cup	**pizza or marinara sauce**
$^1/_3$ cup	**grated mozzarella cheese**
2 tablespoons	**grated Parmesan cheese**
I cup	**favorite pizza toppings**

Turn air fryer to 350 degrees F and place baking sheet in air fryer to preheat for a few minutes.

Lay a sheet of aluminum foil that is the same size as the baking sheet on countertop. Sprinkle cornmeal on top. Lay the pizza dough on top and press flat with hands or rolling pin to about a $^1/_4$-inch thick circle. Brush top of dough with oil. Place foil with dough on top on the heated baking sheet. Bake in air fryer at for 3–5 minutes, until dough is lightly browned.

Remove baking sheet from air fryer and turn dough over. Spread sauce on dough. Spread cheeses and toppings on top of sauce. Bake for another 8–10 minutes, until sauce and cheeses are bubbling. Serve immediately. Makes 2 servings.

SLOPPY JOE BUNDLES

8 ounces	**lean ground beef**
1/2 cup	**finely diced onion**
1/4 cup	**finely diced green bell pepper**
1/3 cup	**ketchup**
1 tablespoon	**apple cider vinegar**
1 tablespoon	**Worcestershire or steak sauce**
1/2 teaspoon	**garlic powder**
1 tube (8 ounces)	**refrigerated crescent roll dough**

Preheat baking sheet in air fryer at 400 degrees F for 10 minutes.

In a medium skillet over medium-high heat cook beef, onion, and bell pepper, breaking up beef into small bits while it cooks. When beef is browned and vegetables are soft, stir in ketchup, vinegar, Worcestershire sauce, and garlic powder. Simmer and stir until most of liquid has evaporated, about 5 minutes. Turn off heat and let cool to warm.

Unroll crescent dough onto a piece of aluminum foil that is the size of the baking sheet. Cut dough into 4 squares. Crimp together any perforations in the dough. Place 1/3 cup beef mixture into center of each dough square. Take 2 opposing corners and bring up over beef mixture in center and pinch dough corners together at top. Repeat for remaining corners.

Turn air fryer to 300 degrees F. Place bundles on foil on top of heated baking sheet. Bake for about 15 minutes, until dough is browned and cooked through. Makes 4 servings.

CUBAN HAM AND SPAM SANDWICHES

I can (12 ounces)	**low-sodium Spam**
I loaf	**country-style white bread**
4 tablespoons	**butter,** softened
4 tablespoons	**yellow mustard**
8 thin slices	**Swiss cheese**
4 thin slices	**deli ham**
2	**large dill pickles,** very thinly sliced

Preheat air fryer to 425 degrees F for about 5 minutes. Slice Spam in very thin slices and place on baking sheet. Bake in air fryer for 3 minutes. Turn slices over and bake another 3 minutes. Remove slices and press with a paper towel to remove excess oil.

Cut bread into 8 slices, a little thicker than $1/4$ inch. Spread butter on I side of each slice and place 4 coated slices, butter side down, on a cutting board. Spread top of slices with mustard. Place on the bread slice in the following order: I slice cheese, ham, cooked Spam slices, pickle slices, and I slice cheese. Spread remaining 4 slices of bread with mustard. Place mustard side down on top.

Place I or 2 sandwiches on baking sheet and bake for 5 minutes. Turn sandwiches over and bake another 3 minutes. Remove from air fryer and place on a dinner plate. Then, place another dinner plate on top for a few minutes and press down gently to compress sandwich. Repeat the process for remaining sandwiches. Serve immediately. Makes 4 servings.

CORN DOG MUFFINS

4	**hot dogs**
I tablespoon	**vegetable oil**
I cup	**flour**
$^1/_2$ cup	**cornmeal**
I teaspoon	**baking powder**
$^1/_2$ teaspoon	**baking soda**
$^1/_4$ teaspoon	**salt**
I tablespoon	**sugar**
$^1/_3$ cup	**sour cream**
$^1/_3$ cup	**milk**
4 tablespoons	**butter,** melted
I	**large egg**
	ketchup and mustard, for serving

Cut hot dogs into $^1/_2$-inch wide half-moon slices. Heat a medium skillet to medium-high heat and add oil and then hot dog slices. Saute until lightly browned on both sides. Let cool.

In a large bowl, whisk together the flour, cornmeal, baking powder, baking soda, salt, and sugar. Stir in sour cream, milk, butter, and egg. Fold in hot dog slices.

Spray a 6-cup jumbo muffin tin or 6 (I-cup) ramekins with cooking oil. Scoop $^1/_2$ cup batter into each cup. Bake in air fryer at 325 degrees F for 15 minutes. Serve warm drizzled with ketchup and mustard. Makes 6 servings.

MEXICAN PIZZAS

3 (6- to 8-inch)	**flour tortillas**
I cup	**refried beans**
2 tablespoons	**sour cream**
I cup	**grated cheddar cheese**
I cup	**toppings of choice, such as sliced green onions, diced green chiles, diced tomatoes, or crumbled queso fresco cheese**

Lightly spray both sides of a tortilla with cooking oil and place on wire basket. Bake in air fryer at 300 degrees for 2 minutes. Remove tortilla from air fryer and place on a flat surface. Prick with a fork in several spots. Gently press tortilla flat with a kitchen towel. Turn tortilla over and place back in wire basket. Bake for another minute. Repeat this process for remaining tortillas.

Stir together the beans and sour cream and microwave for 60 seconds. Stir again. Spread $^1/_3$ cup on each tortilla. Sprinkle cheese evenly over beans. Bake each coated tortilla for another 2 minutes. Scatter toppings over tortillas. Cut into wedges and serve immediately. Makes 3–4 servings.

BARBECUE JACKFRUIT SANDWICHES

I can (14 ounces)	**jackfruit,** drained
1/2 cup	**barbecue sauce**
I cup	**shredded cabbage**
1/2	**red bell pepper,** cut into thin strips
1/4 cup	**grated carrot**
2 tablespoons	**red wine vinegar**
4 tablespoons	**olive oil,** divided
I teaspoon	**sugar**
	salt and pepper, to taste
4	**hamburger buns**

Spread jackfruit out on a cutting board. Using hands, shred jackfruit into pieces and remove any seeds. Pat dry with paper towels. Toss jackfruit with barbecue sauce. Spray baking sheet with cooking oil and scatter jackfruit on baking sheet, leaving space in between clumps.

Bake in air fryer at 400 degrees F for 5 minutes. Stir mixture and bake for another 5 minutes. Stir and bake for about another 5 minutes, until some of the edges of jackfruit are browned.

Toss together the cabbage, bell pepper, carrot, vinegar, 2 tablespoons oil, and sugar. Add salt and pepper.

Brush cut sides of buns with remaining 2 tablespoons of oil and place on baking sheet, cut sides up. Bake in air fryer for about 3 minutes, until lightly browned. Spoon jackfruit onto bottom buns and top with cabbage mixture. Add top buns and serve. Makes 4 servings.

APPETIZERS & SNACKS

WINGS THREE WAYS

10	**chicken wings,** tips removed and separated into wingettes and drumettes
1 tablespoon	**baking powder**
1 teaspoon	**salt**
	glaze, of choice

Dry chicken with a paper towel. Place in a large bowl, and sprinkle with baking powder and salt. Toss until pieces are evenly coated. Line baking sheet with aluminum foil.

Spray wire basket with cooking oil and place on top of baking sheet. Lay the chicken on basket, leaving space between the pieces. Spray with oil. Bake in air fryer at 400 degrees F for 10 minutes. Turn wings over and bake another 8–10 minutes, until lightly browned and crisp.

Toss wings in one of the glazes below. Place coated chicken back on wire basket and bake for another 3 minutes. Makes 4–6 servings.

Classic Buffalo Glaze Stir together 1/4 cup cayenne pepper sauce (such as Frank's), 2 tablespoons brown sugar, and 2 tablespoons melted butter. Heat in microwave until very hot.

Asian Glaze Stir together 1/4 cup Korean gochujang sauce or chili sauce, 2 tablespoons soy sauce, 1 tablespoon honey, and 2 teaspoons sesame oil. Heat in microwave until very hot.

Smoky Apricot Glaze Stir together 1/4 cup apricot jam, 1 tablespoon cayenne pepper sauce (such as Frank's), and 2 teaspoons smoked paprika. Heat in microwave until very hot.

CHEESY KALE CHIPS

I large bunch	**kale**
1/3 cup	**cashews**
1/3 cup	**finely grated Parmesan cheese**
I tablespoon	**lemon juice**
I teaspoon	**lemon zest**
2 tablespoons	**olive oil**
I teaspoon	**cayenne pepper sauce**
	salt and pepper, to taste

Cut stems from kale and then cut leaves into large pieces. You should have 8 cups loosely packed kale.

Place cashews in a microwave-safe bowl and cover with water. Microwave for 2 minutes on high. Let sit for 10 minutes. Drain off water.

Place cashews, Parmesan cheese, lemon juice, lemon zest, oil, and pepper sauce in a blender. Blend for a few seconds. Scrape sides of blender down and add a little water as needed and then blend until very smooth. Mixture should be the consistency of sour cream. Place kale in a large mixing bowl. Add blender mixture and toss to evenly coat.

Spray wire basket with cooking oil, and place coated kale on wire basket in a single layer, leaving space between pieces. Bake in batches as needed in air fryer at 325 degrees F for 5 minutes. While still warm, season with salt and pepper. Chips will crisp up as they cool. Makes 4 servings.

CRISPY SPICED CHICKPEAS

I can (15 ounces)	**chickpeas,** drained and rinsed
I tablespoon	**olive oil**
2 teaspoons	**chili powder**
2 teaspoons	**smoked paprika**
2 teaspoons	**cumin**
I teaspoon	**cornstarch**
	salt and pepper, to taste

Spread chickpeas out on a baking sheet and let sit at least 4 hours, up to overnight.

Toss chickpeas with oil. Mix together chili powder, paprika, cumin, and cornstarch. Toss chickpeas with spice mixture. Spray wire basket generously with cooking oil. Spread coated chickpeas on wire basket in a single layer. Spray with oil.

Bake in air fryer at 350 degrees F for 5 minutes. Remove baking sheet from fryer, shake chickpeas and bake another 5 minutes. While warm, sprinkle with salt and pepper. Makes 2 cups.

VARIATIONS

You can substitute spices to vary the flavors. Some good alternatives:

2 tablespoons Old Bay Seasoning

2 tablespoons Cajun spice blend

I tablespoon Italian herb blend, I teaspoon oregano, 2 teaspoons finely grated Parmesan cheese

I tablespoon curry powder, I teaspoon coriander, I teaspoon cumin

MEXICAN STREET CORN DIP

2 ears	**corn or 2 cups corn kernels**
1	**jalapeno pepper,** seeds removed and minced
2	**green onions,** thinly sliced
1/2 cup	**Mexican crema or sour cream**
1/4 cup	**mayonnaise**
2 tablespoons	**lime juice**
2 teaspoons	**chili powder**
3/4 cup	**crumbled queso fresco or mild feta cheese,** divided
1 teaspoon	**cayenne pepper sauce**
	tortilla chips, for serving

Spray ears of corn with cooking oil and place on baking sheet. If using corn kernels, spread on baking sheet and spray with oil. Bake in air fryer at 450 degrees F for 3 minutes. Turn ears over, or stir kernels. Bake for another 2 minutes. Let cool a bit and then remove kernels from ears of corn.

In an 8-inch round pan, stir cooked kernels with jalapeno, green onions, crema, mayonnaise, lime juice, chili powder, 1/2 cup queso fresco, and pepper sauce. Sprinkle remaining queso fresco on top. Bake in air fryer at 300 degrees F for 8–10 minutes, until lightly browned on top. Serve immediately with chips. Makes 4–6 servings.

BOWTIE CHIPS WITH MARINARA DIP

4 ounces	**large bowtie pasta***
1/2 cup	**finely grated Parmesan cheese**
1 teaspoon	**garlic powder**
1 teaspoon	**Italian seasoning**
1 cup	**marinara sauce**
1/2 cup	**ricotta cheese or cottage cheese**

Boil pasta in salted water for 8–10 minutes, until tender. Stir together Parmesan cheese, garlic powder, and Italian seasoning in a large bowl. Drain pasta, and then toss in bowl with Parmesan mixture.

Spray wire basket with cooking oil. Spread a single layer of coated pasta on wire basket. Spray pasta with oil. Bake in air fryer at 375 degrees F for 10–12 minutes, until lightly browned around edges. Remove pasta to a serving plate. Bake the remaining coated pasta in batches following the same directions.

Place marinara sauce in a glass bowl and microwave for 2 minutes. Stir marinara sauce and swirl in ricotta cheese, leaving in streaks not mixed in with marinara sauce. Microwave for an additional 2 minutes. Serve with pasta chips for dipping. Makes 4–6 servings.

*If bowtie pasta is not available, cook 3 lasagna noodles, cool, and cut into 2-inch-wide pieces and proceed with rest of recipe.

ONION RING TOWER

2	**large Vidalia or other sweet onions**
$1/4$ cup	**cornstarch**
$1/4$ cup	**flour**
I teaspoon	**salt**
2 teaspoons	**chili powder or smoked paprika**
2	**large eggs,** whisked with 2 tablespoons water
I cup	**cornflake crumbs**
$1/3$ cup	**plain Greek yogurt**
2 tablespoons	**mayonnaise**
I tablespoon	**ketchup**
I teaspoon	**Dijon mustard**

Cut onions across diameter in $1/2$-inch sections, separating into rings. Place rings in a bowl and cover with cold water.

In a small shallow bowl, stir together cornstarch, flour, salt, and chili powder. In another bowl, pour egg mixture. In a third shallow bowl, spread cornflake crumbs. Dip wet onion rings into cornstarch mixture, then egg mixture, and then in cornflake crumbs. Spray wire basket with cooking oil and place coated onion rings, separated slightly, on wire basket. Spray generously with oil.

Bake in air fryer at 350 degrees F for 5 minutes. Turn rings over and bake another 5 minutes.

Stir together the yogurt, mayonnaise, ketchup, and mustard. Spoon into a small bowl for dipping. For a fun presentation, stack onion rings on a plate, starting with the largest ring and ending with the smallest, forming a tall tower. Makes 4–6 servings.

CRUSTY AVOCADO WEDGES

2	**ripe but firm avocados**
1/2 cup	**flour**
1 cup	**panko-style breadcrumbs**
1/2 cup	**finely ground Parmesan cheese**
2	**large eggs**
2 tablespoons	**milk**
1/2 cup	**mayonnaise**
1 to 2 tablespoons	**Sriracha or other hot sauce**

Cut avocados in half lengthwise, remove pits, and cut each half into 4 wedges. Remove peels.

Spread flour on a small plate. Mix breadcrumbs and cheese and place in a shallow dish. Whisk eggs and milk in a separate shallow dish.

Spray air fryer basket with cooking oil. Press avocado wedges into flour on all sides, shaking off excess flour. Dip avocado wedges into egg mixture and then into breadcrumb mixture, pressing lightly to ensure that breadcrumbs stick to wedges. Place coated wedges on air fryer basket and then spray with oil.

Bake in air fryer at 350 degrees F for 5–6 minutes, until lightly browned.

Mix together the mayonnaise and Sriracha sauce and serve as a dipping sauce for wedges. Makes 4–6 servings.

PIMIENTO CHEESE JALAPENO POPPERS

4 tablespoons	**cream cheese,** softened
1/2 cup	**grated sharp cheddar cheese**
2 tablespoons	**diced pimientos**
2 teaspoons	**cayenne pepper sauce**
4	**large jalapeno peppers**
1/4 cup	**crushed butter crackers**

Mix together cream cheese, cheddar cheese, pimientos, and pepper sauce. Cut jalapenos in half lengthwise. Using a small spoon, scoop out seeds and pulp. Fill each jalapeno half with cheese mixture. Sprinkle with crushed crackers.

Place on wire basket prepared with cooking oil. Bake in air fryer at 350 degrees F for 8 minutes. Makes 8 servings.

BETTER-THAN-TAKEOUT EGGROLLS

8 ounces	**country-style ground pork sausage**
3 cloves	**garlic,** minced
1 tablespoon	**grated ginger**
2 tablespoons	**soy sauce**
1 bag (16 ounces)	**coleslaw mix (shredded cabbage and carrots)**
12 (6-inch)	**eggroll wrappers**
	spicy mustard or other dipping sauce, optional

In a large skillet over medium-high heat, cook sausage until browned, breaking up into small bits with a fork. Add in garlic, ginger, and soy sauce and cook for another minute. Add coleslaw mix to skillet and stir while cooking to release moisture. When coleslaw mix has wilted and cooked down and most of moisture has evaporated, remove from heat and let cool to warm.

Lay out an egg roll wrapper and spoon $1/4$ cup skillet mixture on top. Wet all 4 edges of wrapper with water. Roll up like you would a burrito, tucking in edges at sides. Repeat using remaining ingredients.

Spray wire basket with cooking oil. Place egg rolls on wire basket and spray with oil. Bake at 325 degrees F for 10 minutes, turning eggrolls over in middle of cooking time. Serve with a spicy mustard dipping sauce, if desired. Makes 4–6 servings.

CRISPY PORK POT STICKERS

3 tablespoons	**vegetable oil,** divided
8 ounces	**ground pork**
2 teaspoons	**grated ginger**
2 teaspoons	**Sriracha or other hot sauce**
1 tablespoon	**soy sauce**
1 teaspoon	**sesame oil**
1	**green onion,** thinly sliced
24	**gyoza or pot sticker wrappers**
1/4 cup	**low-sodium soy sauce**
1/4 cup	**rice vinegar**
1/2 teaspoon	**sugar**

In a medium skillet over medium-high heat, add 1 tablespoon vegetable oil and cook pork about 3 minutes until lightly browned, smashing into small bits with a fork. Add ginger, Sriracha, soy sauce, and sesame oil and cook until most of liquid has evaporated. Turn off heat and stir in green onion.

Lay a gyoza wrapper on a cutting board and spoon 1 tablespoon of pork mixture on the center of the wrapper. Wet a finger and spread a little water all around edge of wrapper. Bring opposite edges up on top of pork and press edges together. Crimp edges together, forming a half-moon purse shape. Repeat for all 24 pot stickers.

Spread remaining 2 tablespoons vegetable oil on a small plate. Dip bottoms of pot stickers in oil and then place on baking sheet. Spray with cooking oil. Bake in air fryer at 400 degrees F for 5 minutes. Stir together low-sodium soy sauce, vinegar, and sugar to use as a dipping sauce. Makes 4 servings.

SPINACH-ARTICHOKE-STUFFED MUSHROOMS

12	**large cremini or white button mushrooms**
3 tablespoons	**olive oil**
4 ounces	**cream cheese,** softened
1 cup	**chopped spinach leaves**
1/2 cup	**grated mozzarella cheese**
1/2 cup	**finely grated Parmesan cheese,** divided
1 jar (6 ounces)	**marinated artichoke hearts,** drained and diced
1 teaspoon	**cayenne pepper sauce**

Using a small spoon, remove stems from mushrooms and scrape out gills. Toss mushrooms with oil and place on wire basket. Bake in air fryer at 375 degrees F for 3 minutes.

Stir together cream cheese, spinach, mozzarella cheese, 1/3 cup Parmesan cheese, artichokes, and pepper sauce. Spoon mixture into caps of mushrooms, pressing down to fill. Sprinkle remaining Parmesan cheese on top. Bake in air fryer for about 12 minutes, until bubbly and browned. Makes 12 servings.

SHEET PAN TOTCHOS

4 cups	**frozen tater tots**
1 cup	**grated pepper jack cheese**
1/2 cup	**grated cheddar cheese**
1 cup	**refried beans**
2 tablespoons	**Mexican crema or sour cream**
1 cup	**nacho toppings of choice** (sliced green onions, diced jalapeno, sliced black olives, etc.)
1/3 cup	**crumbled queso fresco or feta cheese**
	salsa, for serving

Spread tots in a single layer on baking sheet. Bake in air fryer at 350 degrees F for 10 minutes. Turn tots over and bake another 5–8 minutes, checking frequently the last few minutes so as not to burn. Sprinkle pepper jack and cheddar cheese on tots while they are still hot.

In a small glass bowl, stir together the beans and crema. Microwave for 90 seconds or more, until very hot. Stir again and drizzle on top of hot cheese. Place back in air fryer that has been turned off to keep warm until serving.

Just before serving, scatter nacho toppings on top as desired. Sprinkle queso fresco on top. Serve immediately on sheet pan with salsa on the side for serving. Makes 3–4 servings.

EASY BLENDER FALAFEL

I can (15 ounces)	**chickpeas,** drained and rinsed
1/4 cup	**thinly sliced green onions**
I teaspoon	**garlic powder**
I teaspoon	**cumin**
I teaspoon	**coriander**
1/2 teaspoon	**cayenne pepper sauce**
1/2 teaspoon	**baking soda**
2 tablespoons	**extra virgin olive oil**
I tablespoon	**lemon juice**
1/2 cup	**panko-style breadcrumbs**
1/3 cup	**favorite sauce***

Process in food processor or blend in blender, chickpeas, green onions, spices, pepper sauce, baking soda, oil, and lemon juice, until mixture is in small bits, stopping frequently to scrape down sides.

Using a 2-tablespoon scoop for each falafel piece, scoop mixture out and flatten slightly into a disc. Press disc into the breadcrumbs and place on baking sheet prepared with cooking oil.

Spray with oil. Bake in air fryer at 350 degrees F for 10 minutes. Turn falafel pieces over and bake another 5 minutes. Serve drizzled with a favorite sauce. Makes 12 servings.

*For a tasty sauce, try stirring together 1/4 cup mayonnaise, 2 tablespoons ketchup or Sriracha sauce, and 2 tablespoons lemon juice.

SUMPTUOUS
SIDES

SMOKY ACORN SQUASH RINGS

1	**large acorn squash**
2 tablespoons	**maple syrup**
1 tablespoon	**smoked paprika**
1 tablespoon	**soy sauce**

Cut squash into rings that are about $1/2$ inch in diameter. Using a spoon, scoop seeds and strings out of middle of rings.

Spray wire basket with cooking oil. Place rings on wire basket. Mix syrup, paprika, and soy sauce. Brush onto acorn rings. Bake in air fryer at 400 degrees F for 5 minutes.

Turn rings over, brush with more syrup mixture and bake another 5 minutes. Turn rings over and brush with more syrup mixture. Bake another 3–5 minutes, until fork tender. Serve immediately. Makes 4 servings.

SPICY SWEET-GLAZED BRUSSELS SPROUTS

1 tablespoon	**honey**
2 tablespoons	**gochujang,** or other thick spicy sauce
2 tablespoons	**balsamic vinegar**
12	**Brussels sprouts,** cut in half
	salt and pepper, to taste

Stir together honey, gochujang sauce, and vinegar. Toss sprouts in half of sauce mixture. Spray basket with cooking oil. Spread sprouts in a single layer on basket. Bake in air fryer at 400 degrees F for 8 minutes.

Remove sprouts from basket and toss in remaining sauce mixture. Spread in a single layer in basket. Bake for another 4–5 minutes, until fork tender. Sprinkle with salt and pepper. Makes 4 servings.

ASIAN STICKY GREEN BEANS

16 ounces	**green beans,** ends removed
1 tablespoon	**olive oil**
1 teaspoon	**sesame oil**
	salt and pepper, to taste
3 tablespoons	**hoisin sauce**
1 teaspoon	**cayenne pepper sauce**
	sesame seeds, for garnish

Toss beans in oils and sprinkle with a little salt and pepper. Spread beans on wire basket. Bake in air fryer at 450 degrees F for 3 minutes.

Remove beans and toss with hoisin and pepper sauces. Spread in wire basket and bake another 3 minutes. Serve immediately, garnished with sesame seeds. Makes 4–6 servings.

NO-FAIL FRENCH FRIES

I large (12 ounces) **russet potato**
2 tablespoons **olive oil**
salt, to taste

Cut potato lengthwise into long, thin fry shapes. Place in a bowl and cover with cold water. Let sit for about 30 minutes, stirring occasionally. Drain, cover with cold water, and let sit another 30 minutes. Pat potatoes dry with a paper towel.

Toss fries with oil. Arrange on wire basket so that fries are not crowded. Bake in air fryer at 400 degrees F for about 12 minutes, watching closely at end of cooking time so as not to burn. Check fries. If not crispy enough, cook 1 more minute at a time until very crispy. Cooking time varies according to how thick fries are cut. Season with salt and serve immediately. Makes 2 servings.

THE ULTIMATE CHEESY GARLIC BREAD

1 large loaf (about 12 inches) **French bread**
$^1/_2$ cup **butter,** room temperature
5 cloves **garlic,** pressed or finely grated
$^1/_3$ cup **finely grated Parmesan cheese**

Slice bread into 1-inch-thick slices. Place slices on a flat surface.

Mix the butter, garlic, and cheese. Spread a $^1/_4$-inch layer of butter mixture on top side of each of the slices of bread.

Place several slices in wire basket and bake in air fryer at 400 degrees F for 5 minutes, until lightly browned. Repeat for remaining slices. Serve immediately. Makes 12 slices.

DUCHESS POTATOES

16 ounces	**russet potatoes,** unpeeled
1/2 teaspoon	**salt**
1/2 cup	**grated sharp white cheddar cheese**
2 tablespoons	**cream cheese,** softened
1/4 teaspoon	**nutmeg**
2	**large eggs**
3 tablespoons	**butter,** melted

Cut potatoes in half lengthwise. Spray baking sheet with cooking oil. Place potatoes, cut sides down, on baking sheet. Bake in air fryer at 375 degrees F for 30 minutes. Remove potatoes from air fryer and let cool a bit. While still very warm, peel off skins and cut potatoes into chunks. Use a ricer to rice potatoes or use a food processor to break up into small bits. Stir in salt and cheese, mixing until cheese melts into potatoes. Stir in cream cheese, nutmeg, and eggs.

Spoon potato mixture into a piping bag with a star tip or a large zip top bag with a hole cut into 1 corner. Chill for at least 30 minutes, or up to 24 hours. Pipe potato mixture into circles that are about 1/2 cup each and about 1 inch thick.

Brush potato circles with butter. Bake in air fryer at 400 degrees F for 10–12 minutes, until lightly browned. Makes 6 servings.

GARLIC-PARMESAN BROCCOLI

4 cups	**small broccoli florets**
2 tablespoons	**olive oil**
1/2 teaspoon	**salt**
1/2 teaspoon	**pepper**
2 cloves	**garlic,** minced
1 tablespoon	**lemon juice**
3 tablespoons	**grated Parmesan cheese**

Toss broccoli in oil, salt, and pepper. Spread in a single layer on baking sheet. Bake in air fryer at 400 degrees F for 5 minutes. Toss broccoli with garlic. Bake for another 2 minutes.

In a medium serving bowl, toss hot broccoli with lemon juice and cheese. Serve immediately. Makes 4 servings.

CURRIED
CAULIFLOWER STEAKS

1 large head	**cauliflower**
3 tablespoons	**olive oil,** divided
1 teaspoon	**each salt and pepper,** divided
2 tablespoons	**curry powder**
1/4 cup	**minced parsley**
1/2 cup	**minced toasted walnuts**
1 teaspoon	**lemon zest**

With the stem on the bottom, place cauliflower on a cutting board and cut in half. Cut 4 (1-inch-thick) slices from the center and largest part of cauliflower, including the stem. Reserve the remaining pieces of cauliflower for another use. Using 2 tablespoons of oil, brush both sides of the 4 slices with oil. Sprinkle both sides with 3/4 teaspoon each of salt and pepper. Sprinkle both sides of cauliflower slices with curry powder.

Place cauliflower slices on baking sheet. If necessary, bake in batches. Bake in air fryer at 325 degrees F for 15 minutes. Turn over and bake for another 10 minutes.

Meanwhile, stir together the parsley, walnuts, zest, remaining oil, and remaining salt and pepper. Serve this mixture on top of cauliflower slices. Makes 4 servings.

CRISPY CRASH POTATOES

12	**petite red potatoes,** each the size of a golf ball
2 tablespoons	**minced herbs,** such as rosemary or thyme
4 tablespoons	**butter,** melted
	salt and pepper, to taste
	garnishes as desired, such as sour cream, minced chives, crumbled bacon, or bleu cheese

Bring a stockpot full of salted water to a boil. Add potatoes and cook for 8–10 minutes, until fork tender.

Spray baking sheet with cooking oil. Place cooked potatoes on baking sheet about 1 inch apart. You may need to bake in batches. Take a glass or a measuring cup and flatten each potato to about $1/2$-inch thickness. Stir herbs into butter and drizzle onto each flattened potato. Sprinkle with salt and pepper. Bake in air fryer at 450 degrees F for 10–12 minutes, until browned and crispy. Serve immediately with garnishes as desired. Makes 4 servings.

LOADED BAKED CAULIFLOWER

4 cups	**cauliflower florets**
2 tablespoons	**butter,** melted
1/2 teaspoon	**salt**
1/2 teaspoon	**pepper**
1/2 cup	**grated cheddar cheese**
1/4 cup	**sour cream**
1/2 cup	**cooked crumbled bacon**
1	**green onion,** thinly sliced

Cut any large florets in half so that pieces are roughly the same size. Toss florets in butter, sprinkle with salt and pepper and spread on baking sheet. Bake in air fryer at 400 degrees F for 12–15 minutes, until fork tender and lightly browned.

While still hot, sprinkle cooked cauliflower with cheese. Place in a serving bowl. Drizzle sour cream on top. Scatter bacon and green onions on top. Serve immediately. Makes 4–6 servings.

RED BLISS
HASSLEBACK POTATOES

6	**red bliss potatoes,** each about the size of a tennis ball
3 tablespoons	**butter,** melted
$^1/_2$ teaspoon	**salt**
$^1/_2$ teaspoon	**pepper**
	dash of cayenne pepper sauce
	sour cream and minced chives, for serving

Place a potato on a cutting board, cutting a thin slice off bottom of potato as necessary to make sure potato remains stable. Place a chopstick or butter knife next to each side of the potato. Make slices that are $^1/_4$-inch thick through whole potato, stopping at chopsticks so you are not cutting through potato at bottom. Potatoes should fan out slightly. Repeat for each potato.

Place potatoes on baking sheet. Mix butter, salt, pepper, and pepper sauce together. Using a pastry brush to get into cuts on potatoes, brush with half of the butter mixture. Bake in air fryer at 350 degrees F for 10 minutes.

Remove baking sheet from air fryer and brush potatoes with remaining butter mixture. Bake for another 10–12 minutes, until potatoes are fork tender. Serve immediately with sour cream and chives. Makes 6 servings.

BEEF & PORK MAIN DISHES

QUICK CARNE ASADA

I	**jalapeno pepper,** stem and seeds removed and finely diced
3 cloves	**garlic,** minced
$^1/_2$	**small red onion,** diced
2 tablespoons	**lime juice**
3 tablespoons	**Worcestershire sauce**
I tablespoon	**cayenne pepper sauce**
3 tablespoons	**olive oil**
I teaspoon	**salt**
I (18- to 24-ounce)	**flank steak**
I tablespoon	**brown sugar**
2 tablespoons	**chili powder**

Using a large zip top bag, add jalapeno, garlic, onion, lime juice, Worcestershire sauce, pepper sauce, olive oil, and salt, and shake to combine. Cover flank steak with plastic wrap and pound to a uniform I-inch thickness. Add flank steak to bag and let sit on counter I hour, turning occasionally.

Remove steak from bag and wipe clean. Pat steak dry with paper towels. Mix brown sugar and chili powder together. Coat I side of steak with half of chili powder mixture. Spray basket with cooking oil and place steak, coated side up, in basket.

Bake in air fryer at 400 degrees F for 5 minutes. Turn steak over and coat other side with remaining chili powder mixture. Bake for another 5 minutes.

Let steak rest for 5 minutes then slice thinly across grain. Serve alone or in tacos, burritos, or rice bowls. Makes 4–6 servings.

SHEPHERD'S PIE
TWICE-BAKED POTATOES

3	**large russet potatoes,** cut in half lengthwise
2 tablespoons	**olive oil,** divided
1 teaspoon	**each salt and pepper,** divided
1/2	**medium yellow onion,** finely diced
12 ounces	**lean ground beef**
2 tablespoons	**Worcestershire sauce**
1/4 cup	**ketchup**
2 tablespoons	**tomato paste**
1 teaspoon	**cayenne pepper sauce**
1/2 cup	**beef broth**
1 cup	**frozen peas and diced carrots**
2 tablespoons	**butter,** melted
1/3 cup	**heavy cream**

Brush potatoes with 1 tablespoon oil. Sprinkle with 1/2 teaspoon each salt and pepper. Place on baking sheet and bake in air fryer at 375 degrees F for 30 minutes. Remove and let cool to warm. Scoop out flesh of potato halves, leaving a 1/4-inch shell.

Saute remaining oil and onion over medium-high heat until onion is softened, about 3 minutes. Add beef and cook until browned, breaking up into small bits. Stir in Worcestershire sauce, ketchup, tomato paste, pepper sauce, broth, and peas and carrots. Let simmer until most of liquid has evaporated. Spoon skillet mixture into potato shells.

Place reserved potato flesh in a mixing bowl. Add remaining salt and pepper, butter, and cream and mix on medium-high speed until fluffy, adding a little water as necessary to lighten. Spoon potatoes onto tops of filled potato shells. Bake in air fryer at 350 degrees F for 10–12 minutes until browned and bubbly. Makes 6 servings.

CHIMICHURRI SKIRT STEAK

1 cup	**chopped fresh parsley leaves**
2 tablespoons	**diced shallot**
1/2 tablespoon	**minced jalapeno pepper**
1 large clove	**garlic,** diced
3 tablespoons	**red wine vinegar**
3 tablespoons	**olive oil**
1/2 teaspoon	**salt**
1/2 teaspoon	**pepper**
1 (24-ounce)	**skirt steak,** at room temperature*
2 tablespoons	**butter**

Pulse parsley, shallot, jalapeno, and garlic in food processor until everything is in small bits. Place in a small bowl and stir in vinegar, oil, salt, and pepper and let sit for at least 10 minutes so flavors blend.

Preheat air fryer with baking sheet inside at 450 degrees F for 10 minutes. Cut visible fat from steak and pat dry with paper towels. Cut steak into pieces as needed to fit baking sheet. Spread butter on both sides of steak. Bake in air fryer for 6 minutes for medium-rare steak. Turn over and bake another 2 minutes. Remove from air fryer and let rest 15 minutes. Cut into thin slices across the grain. Serve with chimichurri spooned over top of slices, or on the side. Makes 4 servings.

*If skirt steak is not available, ribeye steaks are a good substitute.

TUESDAY NIGHT
BEEF BULGOGI

2 pounds	**ribeye or sirloin steak**
$^1/_2$	**ripe pear,** grated
$^1/_4$ cup	**low-sodium soy sauce**
2 tablespoons	**brown sugar**
1 tablespoon	**sesame oil**
5 cloves	**garlic,** minced
2 tablespoons	**grated ginger**
2 tablespoons	**gochujang or other hot sauce**
2 tablespoons	**vegetable oil**
	thinly sliced green onions and sesame seeds, for garnish

Trim excess visible fat from steaks. Slice steak in $^1/_4$-inch slices across the grain.

Using a large zip top bag, add the pear, soy sauce, brown sugar, sesame oil, garlic, ginger, gochujang sauce, and vegetable oil and shake to combine. Add the steak and let sit on counter for about 30 minutes, turning occasionally.

While steak is marinating, preheat air fryer to 450 degrees F with baking sheet inside for 5 minutes.

Remove steak from marinade and shake off strips to remove excess marinade while placing them on the heated baking sheet. Bake in air fryer for 2 minutes. Remove baking sheet, turn steak over, and cook another 1−2 minutes until lightly browned around edges. Sprinkle with green onions and sesame seeds and serve immediately. Makes 4 servings.

PIZZA SUPREME-
STUFFED PEPPERS

4 ounces	**hot or sweet Italian sausage,** casings removed
1/2	**onion,** diced
12 slices	**pepperoni,** chopped
1 cup	**cooked brown or white rice**
1/2 cup	**grated mozzarella cheese**
1 can (2 ounces)	**sliced black olives,** drained
1 cup	**marinara sauce**
1/2 cup	**grated Parmesan cheese,** divided
3	**large bell peppers,** any color

In a large skillet, cook sausage over medium-high heat until just cooked through, breaking up into small bits. Add in onion and cook until onion is soft and sausage is browned. Turn off heat and stir in rice, mozzarella cheese, olives, marinara sauce, and 1/4 cup Parmesan cheese.

Cut peppers in half lengthwise and scoop out seeds and pulp. Fill peppers with skillet mixture, pressing down with spoon as you fill. Top stuffed peppers with remaining Parmesan cheese.

Bake in air fryer at 350 degrees F for 18 minutes. Serve immediately. Makes 6 servings.

SHORTCUT CALZONES

12 ounces	**pizza dough**
4 ounces	**mild or sweet Italian sausage**
$^1/_2$	**medium onion,** diced
4	**large cremini mushrooms,** diced
2 cups	**chopped spinach leaves**
1 cup	**marinara sauce,** plus additional for dipping
1 cup	**grated mozzarella cheese**
$^1/_4$ cup	**finely grated Parmesan cheese**

Place pizza dough in a large oiled bowl and cover with a kitchen towel. Set in a warm place for about 1 hour until double in size.

In a large skillet over medium-high heat, saute sausage until browned, breaking up into small bits. Add onion and cook for another 3 minutes. Add mushrooms and cook another minute. Turn off heat and add spinach, marinara sauce, and cheeses.

Cut dough into 6 pieces. Roll each piece out to $^1/_4$-inch thickness in a square shape. Place $^1/_3$ cup skillet mixture in center of each square. Fold 1 corner up over the filling to meet the opposite corner. Press edges together with fingers or with a fork.

Spray wire basket with cooking oil. Place calzones in basket. Bake in air fryer at 350 degrees F for 8 minutes. Turn calzones over and bake another 4 minutes. Serve immediately with heated marinara dipping sauce. Makes 4–6 servings.

MISO AND HONEY-GLAZED PORK CHOPS

3 tablespoons	**white or red miso paste**
2 tablespoons	**honey**
I tablespoon	**sesame oil**
$1/2$ teaspoon	**ground ginger**
I teaspoon	**garlic powder**
2 teaspoons	**soy sauce**
4 (6-ounce)	**pork loin chops**

Mix together miso paste, honey, sesame oil, ginger, garlic, and soy sauce. Rub chops with half of this mixture and place on wire basket. Bake in air fryer at 375 degrees F for 8 minutes.

Turn chops over and spread remaining miso mixture on top sides of chops. Bake for another 2–3 minutes, until glaze is lightly browned. Serve immediately. Makes 4 servings.

ITALIAN MINI MEATLOAVES

$^1/_2$ cup	**Italian breadcrumbs**
$^1/_2$ cup	**milk**
1	**large egg**
$^1/_4$ cup	**finely grated Parmesan cheese**
$^1/_2$ teaspoon	**garlic powder**
6 tablespoons	**sun-dried tomato pesto,** divided
16 ounces	**lean ground beef**
12	**mozzarella pearls,** each the size of a large marble

In a large bowl, whisk breadcrumbs and milk together. Stir in egg, Parmesan cheese, garlic powder, and 2 tablespoons pesto. Using clean hands, mix in ground beef.

Place $^1/_2$ cup beef mixture onto oiled baking sheet. Pat into a rectangular shape, about 2 inches wide and 3 $^1/_2$ inches long. Press 3 mozzarella pearls into rectangle in a line in center. Scoop $^1/_4$ cup more meat mixture onto top of pearls and pat out to cover pearls and form top of mini meatloaf. Repeat process for remaining 3 meatloaves.

Spoon 1 tablespoon pesto on top of each mini meatloaf, spreading over all the tops. Bake in air fryer at 350 degrees F for 15 minutes. Let sit for 5 minutes. Serve immediately. Makes 4 servings.

MARINATED PORK TENDERLOIN

1/4 cup	**olive oil**
1/4 cup	**soy sauce**
2 tablespoons	**orange juice**
2 tablespoons	**brown sugar**
1 tablespoon	**Worcestershire sauce**
1 tablespoon	**Dijon mustard**
1 (2-pound)	**pork tenderloin**
1 tablespoon	**cornstarch**
1/4 cup	**water**

Mix together the oil, soy sauce, orange juice, brown sugar, Worcestershire sauce, and mustard.

Cut pork in half widthwise. Place pork in a large zip top bag and pour in marinade. Refrigerate for 8 hours up to overnight, turning occasionally. Remove pork from bag and place on wire basket. Bake in air fryer at 425 degrees F for 10 minutes.

Pour marinade into a saucepan. Stir cornstarch into water and whisk into saucepan. While pork is cooking, simmer liquid in saucepan for a few minutes until thickened.

Turn pork over and brush with sauce. Bake another 10 minutes. Turn pork over again and brush with sauce. Bake another 10 minutes.

Remove pork and let rest for 10 minutes. Slice pork in 1/2-inch slices and serve drizzled with sauce. Makes 4–6 servings.

BALSAMIC STEAK AND VEGGIE BUNDLES

16 ounces	**sirloin steak,** cut into $^1/_4$-inch-thick large planks, called skillet steaks
3 tablespoons	**Worcestershire sauce**
1 teaspoon	**salt**
$^1/_2$	**red bell pepper**
$^1/_2$	**red onion**
16 thin stalks	**asparagus**
4	**green onions**
$^1/_2$ cup	**balsamic vinegar**
2 tablespoons	**brown sugar**
2 tablespoons	**butter**

Place steak slices in a zip top bag and add Worcestershire sauce and salt, massaging to distribute. Refrigerate for at least 2 hours. Remove meat from marinade and cut steak into 8 strips that are 3 inches wide.

Cut vegetables into 4-inch-long, $^1/_4$-inch-thick pieces. Microwave bell pepper, onion, and asparagus for 60 seconds or more as needed to soften vegetables a little.

Simmer the vinegar and brown sugar until thickened slightly, about 2 minutes. Turn off heat and stir in butter.

Wrap a few bell pepper strips, onion strips, asparagus, and green onion pieces with a slice of beef. Secure with a toothpick. Place on baking sheet. Bake in air fryer at 400 degrees F for 8 minutes. Brush generously with balsamic syrup and bake another 3 minutes. Makes 4–6 servings.

ITALIAN ZUCCHINI SPIRALS

2 (12-ounce)	**zucchini**
$1/2$ cup	**ricotta**
2 ounces	**prosciutto,** cut into paper-thin slices
4 ounces	**mozzarella cheese,** cut into thin slices
2 cups	**marinara sauce,** divided

Slice the zucchini in long planks a little thicker than $1/4$ inch. Place zucchini planks on a plate and cover with plastic wrap. Microwave zucchini for 90 seconds. Test zucchini to see if it is softened and pliable. If necessary, microwave for another 20 seconds at a time until zucchini is pliable. Let cool to warm.

Place a zucchini plank on a flat surface. Spread 1 tablespoon ricotta on zucchini plank. Cut prosciutto into strips to fit zucchini and lay strips on top of ricotta. Cut mozzarella slices to fit zucchini and lay slices on top of prosciutto. Roll up the slices to form a small spiral. Repeat for remaining zucchini.

Spread 1 cup marinara sauce in an 8-inch pie pan, and add zucchini, spiral sides facing up. Spoon remaining marinara sauce on tops of each spiral. Bake in air fryer at 325 degrees F for about 25 minutes, until bubbly. Serve immediately. Makes 4–6 servings.

POULTRY
MAIN DISHES

CRISPY SKIN TURKEY BREAST

1 (2.5–3 pound)	**turkey breast**
4 tablespoons	**butter,** room temperature
$1/2$ tablespoon	**poultry seasoning**
1 teaspoon	**salt**
$1/2$ teaspoon	**pepper**

Place turkey on a cutting board and slide fingers under skin to loosen and separate from turkey. Mix together butter, poultry seasoning, salt, and pepper. Scoop up butter mixture with fingers and rub evenly under the turkey skin. Stretch out skin to cover entire top of turkey and secure at edges with a few toothpicks.

Place turkey in wire basket. Bake in air fryer at 350 degrees F for 35–40 minutes, until meat thermometer shows turkey to be at 160 degrees F. Let rest 10 minutes before slicing and serving. Makes 6–8 servings.

PICKLE-BRINED
AIR-FRIED CHICKEN

1 cup	**brine from a jar of dill pickles**
6	**skinless chicken pieces***
2/3 cup	**flour**
1/3 cup	**cornstarch**
2 teaspoons	**salt,** divided
1 teaspoon	**baking powder**
1	**large egg**
1/2 cup	**buttermilk**
1 tablespoon	**cayenne pepper sauce**
1 cup	**panko-style breadcrumbs**

Marinate chicken in pickle brine for at least 4 hours, up to overnight. The longer the chicken marinates, the more pickle flavor it will have.

In a shallow pan, mix together flour, cornstarch, 1 teaspoon salt, and baking powder. In a separate shallow pan, mix together egg, buttermilk, pepper sauce, and remaining salt. Pour breadcrumbs in a third shallow pan.

Remove chicken from brine with tongs and let excess brine drip off. Dip each chicken piece in flour mixture and then in egg mixture, coating all sides completely. Press chicken in breadcrumbs, making sure each piece is well coated. Let sit on counter for 30 minutes.

Spray wire basket with cooking oil. Place chicken in basket and spray generously with oil. Bake in air fryer at 350 degrees F for 15 minutes. Turn chicken pieces over and spray with oil. Bake for another 15 minutes or so until chicken is browned and cooked through. Makes 4–6 servings.

*If using chicken breasts, cut in half across the width of the breast to make 2 large chunks.

SANTA FE CHICKEN CASSEROLE

I can (15 ounces)	**black beans,** drained and rinsed
1/2 cup	**corn kernels**
1/2	**red bell pepper,** diced
2	**green onions,** thinly sliced
I can (4 ounces)	**diced green chiles or jalapenos,** divided
I cup	**grated Monterey jack cheese,** divided
I cup	**grated sharp cheddar cheese,** divided
I cup	**salsa or red enchilada sauce,** divided
2	**boneless, skinless chicken breasts**
I cup	**crumbs of tortilla chips or corn chips**

In a large bowl, stir together beans, corn, bell pepper, green onions, 1/2 green chiles, 1/2 of each cheese, and all but 2 tablespoons of salsa. Spoon mixture into an 8-inch round pie pan.

Place chicken breasts on a cutting board. With a large knife parallel to the cutting board, slice breasts in half, forming 4 large planks. Place chicken pieces into the bean mixture, nestling down into mixture so that only the tops of the chicken are exposed. Spoon the remaining salsa on tops of chicken.

Bake in air fryer at 325 degrees F for 25 minutes. Scatter remaining green chiles and cheese on top. Bake for another 5 minutes. Let sit for a few minutes and then serve with tortilla crumbs sprinkled on each serving. Makes 4–6 servings.

3 Ms CHICKEN THIGHS

6	**chicken thighs**
2 tablespoons	**vegetable oil**
$^1/_3$ cup	**spicy brown mustard**
3 tablespoons	**maple syrup**
2 tablespoons	**molasses**
$^1/_2$ tablespoon	**cayenne pepper sauce**

Remove skin from chicken pieces or leave skin on, your choice. Brush the skinless sides of chicken with oil. Place chicken, skin side up, on wire basket. Mix together the mustard, maple syrup, molasses, and pepper sauce. Brush a generous coating on top of each chicken piece, using about $^1/_3$ of mixture.

Bake in air fryer at 375 degrees F for 10 minutes. Brush tops of chicken pieces with more sauce mixture. Bake another 8 minutes. Brush tops of chicken pieces with sauce mixture, using all of remaining sauce. Bake another 5 minutes. Let chicken rest for 5 minutes before serving. Makes 6 servings.

CREAMY TINGA TAQUITOS

8	**corn tortillas**
3 tablespoons	**vegetable oil**
2 cups	**shredded cooked chicken,** in small bits
3 tablespoons	**cream cheese,** softened
2	**green onions,** thinly sliced
2	**chipotle peppers from a can,** minced, with a little of their sauce*
	guacamole, if desired, for serving
	salsa, if desired, for serving

Place corn tortillas on baking sheet, overlapping as needed to fit pan. Generously brush both sides of tortillas with oil. Bake in air fryer at 300 degrees F for 2 minutes, to soften tortillas.

Stir together chicken, cream cheese, green onions, and chipotle peppers. Spoon 1/4 cup chicken mixture onto each tortilla. Roll up in a cigar shape. Place taquitos, seam side down, on wire basket. Spray with cooking oil. Bake in air fryer at 375 degrees F for 10 minutes. Serve immediately with guacamole and/or salsa for dipping. Makes 4 servings.

*To decrease the heat level of chipotle peppers, cut them in half and scrape out and discard the seeds.

CHICKEN SATAY SKEWERS WITH PEANUT SAUCE

2	**large boneless, skinless chicken breasts**
3 tablespoons	**soy sauce,** divided
3 cloves	**garlic,** minced
2 tablespoons	**grated ginger,** divided
2 tablespoons	**brown sugar,** divided
1 tablespoon	**fish sauce**
2 tablespoons	**vegetable oil**
$1/4$ cup	**creamy peanut butter**
1 tablespoon	**light corn syrup**
1 tablespoon	**lime juice**
1 tablespoon	**Sriracha or other hot sauce**

Cut chicken into 2-inch chunks and place in a large zip top bag. Whisk together 2 tablespoons soy sauce, garlic, 1 1/2 tablespoons ginger, 1 tablespoon brown sugar, fish sauce, and vegetable oil. Pour into bag with chicken, massaging with hands to distribute marinade. Let sit on countertop for 30 minutes, turning occasionally.

While chicken is marinating, stir together peanut butter, remaining soy sauce, remaining ginger, remaining brown sugar, corn syrup, lime juice, and Sriracha sauce.

Remove chicken from marinade and place on skewers. Pat dry with paper towels. Place on wire basket, spray with cooking oil, and bake in air fryer at 450 degrees F for 10 minutes, turning skewers over halfway through cooking. Warm the peanut sauce in microwave oven. Serve immediately. Makes 4 servings.

RITZY CHICKEN TENDERS

I cup	**finely grated Parmesan cheese**
I cup	**finely crushed Ritz crackers**
16 ounces	**chicken tenders**
$^1/_3$ cup	**mayonnaise**
I teaspoon	**lemon-pepper seasoning**

Mix the cheese and cracker crumbs in a shallow pan or plate. Lay chicken tenders on a flat surface and trim off visible fat and any tendons.

Mix mayonnaise and lemon-pepper seasoning. Brush all sides of chicken with mayonnaise mixture. Press all sides of coated chicken into the crumb mixture. Spray wire basket with cooking oil. Place coated chicken pieces on basket. Bake in air fryer at 350 degrees F for 12 minutes. Serve immediately. Makes 4 servings.

INSIDE-OUT
CHICKEN CORDON BLEU

2 (6-ounce)	**boneless, skinless chicken breasts**
1 cup	**grated Swiss cheese**
4	**large deli ham slices,** cut $^1/_8$ inch thick
2 tablespoons	**mayonnaise**
2 tablespoons	**Dijon mustard**
1 tablespoon	**honey**
$^1/_3$ cup	**dry breadcrumbs**

Lay chicken breasts on a flat surface. With knife parallel to surface cut breasts in half, leaving 2 large flat planks. Cover planks with plastic wrap and pound lightly until planks are uniformly $^1/_2$ inch thick.

Spread cheese on chicken and then wrap each chicken plank and cheese with 1 slice of ham. Mix together the mayonnaise, mustard, and honey. Place wrapped chicken on baking sheet that has been sprayed with a little cooking oil. Brush tops and sides of chicken with mayonnaise mixture. Sprinkle breadcrumbs over tops of chicken bundles until tops are well coated.

Bake in air fryer at 400 degrees F for 8 minutes. Serve immediately. Makes 4 servings.

TANDOORI CHICKEN THIGHS

6	**boneless, skinless chicken thighs**
1/2 cup	**plain yogurt**
1 tablespoon	**minced garlic**
1 tablespoon	**grated ginger**
1 tablespoon	**lime juice**
2 tablespoons	**olive oil**
1 tablespoon	**each garam masala, cumin, chili powder, curry powder, and smoked paprika**
1 teaspoon	**salt**

Open each piece of chicken so that it is lying flat on a cutting board. Remove visible fat. Combine yogurt, garlic, ginger, lime juice, and oil, and then stir in chicken to coat. Cover and refrigerate for at least 2 hours, up to overnight.

Remove chicken from marinade, shaking to remove most of marinade. Lay pieces flat on wire basket with space in between chicken pieces. Cook in 2 or more batches as needed. Bake at 450 degrees F in air fryer for 8 minutes. Turn chicken over, sprinkle with spice mixture and salt, and cook another 2–3 minutes, until charred in spots. Serve immediately. Makes 4–6 servings.

LASAGNA-STUFFED CHICKEN BREASTS

4	**boneless, skinless chicken breasts**
$1/2$ cup	**ricotta cheese**
1	**large egg**
1 teaspoon	**Italian seasoning**
1 teaspoon	**garlic powder**
$1/4$ cup	**finely grated Parmesan cheese**
1 cup	**grated mozzarella cheese,** divided
$1 1/2$ cups	**marinara sauce,** divided

Lay chicken breasts on a cutting board. Holding a large knife parallel to the board, cut chicken breasts through the center almost all the way through. Lay chicken breasts open, so that each breast is like a book.

Mix together the ricotta cheese, egg, Italian seasoning, garlic powder, Parmesan cheese, and $1/2$ of mozzarella cheese. Spread mixture evenly over $1/2$ of each chicken breast. Fold the bare half up over the top of the cheese mixture, covering the mixture.

Spread $1/2$ cup marinara sauce on baking sheet. Lay chicken breast bundles on top. Spoon remaining sauce on tops of chicken. Sprinkle remaining mozzarella cheese on tops of chicken. Bake in air fryer at 350 degrees F for 25 minutes. Serve immediately. Makes 4 servings.

HOT-HONEY CHICKEN

2 teaspoons	**garlic powder**
1 tablespoon	**chili powder**
1 tablespoon	**cumin**
1 tablespoon	**smoked paprika**
1 teaspoon	**salt**
4	**boneless, skinless chicken thighs**
1/3 cup	**honey**
2 tablespoons	**cayenne pepper sauce**

Combine garlic powder, chili powder, cumin, paprika, and salt in a medium bowl. Add chicken thighs and toss well to coat evenly. Spray wire basket with cooking oil. Place chicken thighs on wire basket and spray with oil. Bake in air fryer at 400 degrees F for 5 minutes. Turn chicken over, spray with oil and bake another 2 minutes.

Mix together the honey and pepper sauce. Brush tops of chicken generously, using half of honey mixture. Bake another minute. Turn chicken over and brush generously with remaining honey mixture. Bake another minute. Serve immediately. Makes 4 servings.

WEEKNIGHT CHICKEN ADOBO

4	**chicken thighs**
6 cloves	**garlic,** smashed
1	**jalapeno pepper,** cut in half lengthwise
4	**bay leaves**
3/4 cup	**rice vinegar**
1/2 cup	**low-sodium soy sauce**
2 tablespoons	**brown sugar**
2 tablespoons	**ketchup**
1/2 cup	**coconut milk**
1 tablespoon	**cornstarch**
4 cups	**hot cooked rice**

Place chicken, skin side up, in an 8-inch round pan. Bake in air fryer at 400 degrees F for 10 minutes.

Turn chicken over and place garlic, jalapeno, and bay leaves randomly in spaces between chicken pieces. Stir together vinegar, soy sauce, brown sugar, and ketchup. Pour liquid mixture into pan around chicken, using only enough of liquid mixture so that tops of chicken are without liquid. Bake in air fryer for 10 minutes.

Remove pan from air fryer and turn chicken pieces over so that the skin sides are up and 1/4 inch above liquid mixture. Bake in air fryer for another 15 minutes. Place chicken pieces on serving plates.

Strain liquid and discard solids. Pour strained liquid back into pan. Stir coconut milk and cornstarch together and whisk into pan sauce. Bake for 1 minute at a time, whisking after every minute until mixture is thickened. Spoon rice onto serving plates next to chicken and spoon sauce on top of rice. Makes 4 servings.

SEAFOOD
MAIN DISHES

SHEET PAN SHRIMP BOIL

16 ounces	**baby Yukon gold potatoes**
8 ounces	**large raw shrimp,** peeled and deveined
4 tablespoons	**butter,** melted
3 cloves	**garlic,** minced
1 tablespoon	**Old Bay Seasoning**
8 ounces	**andouille sausage,** cut in $^1/_2$-inch-wide half-moon slices
1 ear	**corn,** cut in 1-inch slices or 1 cup frozen corn
2 tablespoons	**lemon juice**
2 tablespoons	**chopped parsley**

Cut potatoes into 2-inch chunks. Place in a glass dish, cover with plastic wrap, and microwave for about 5 minutes, stirring halfway through, until chunks are fork tender.

Combine shrimp, butter, garlic, and seasoning and let sit while potatoes are cooking. Toss the cooked potatoes, sausage, and corn with the shrimp mixture. Spray baking pan with cooking oil. Spread mixture in a single layer on baking pan.

Bake in air fryer at 350 degrees F for 8 minutes. Spoon mixture onto a platter and sprinkle with lemon juice and parsley. Serve warm. Makes 4 servings.

COCONUT, CASHEW, AND CURRY COD

2 teaspoons	**salt,** divided
4 (6-ounce) fillets	**skinless cod**
2 tablespoons	**mayonnaise**
I tablespoon	**Dijon mustard**
2 tablespoons	**curry powder,** divided
1/2 cup	**unsweetened coconut flakes,** diced
1/2 cup	**roasted, salted cashew pieces,** diced
2 tablespoons	**olive oil**

Sprinkle I teaspoon salt on all sides of fillets. Mix the mayonnaise and mustard together. Spread a thin layer of mayonnaise mixture on I side of fillets. Sprinkle I tablespoon curry powder on coated sides of fillets. Spray baking sheet with cooking oil. Place fillets, coated sides up, on baking sheet. Bake in air fryer at 300 degrees F for 8 minutes. Remove fillets to a serving plate and wipe off baking sheet.

Mix together coconut flakes, cashews, remaining curry powder, and olive oil. Scatter the coconut mixture on the baking sheet and bake for I minute. Stir coconut mixture and bake for about I more minute, until lightly browned.

Spread coconut mixture on top of fillets and serve warm. Makes 4 servings.

SALMON CROQUETTES

1	**(12-ounce) russet potato**
2	**green onions,** thinly sliced
1	**large egg**
1/3 cup	**mayonnaise**
2 teaspoons	**Dijon mustard**
2 teaspoons	**Old Bay seasoning**
1/2 cup	**butter cracker crumbs,** divided
1 can (14 ounces)	**pink salmon,** drained and bones removed
2 tablespoons	**finely grated Parmesan cheese**
	tartar sauce, for serving

Cut potato in half and spray with a little cooking oil. Bake in air fryer at 400 degrees F for about 30 minutes, until very tender. Let cool. Peel and smash into small bits with a fork.

Place potato in a large bowl and stir in green onions, egg, mayonnaise, mustard, Old Bay seasoning, and 1/4 cup cracker crumbs. Carefully stir in salmon, leaving in small chunks. Form mixture into 6 round croquette patties that are a scant 1/2 cup each and 1 inch thick.

Mix remaining cracker crumbs and cheese together in a shallow dish. Press croquettes into mixture, coating both sides. Refrigerate for 20 minutes.

Spray wire basket with oil. Place croquettes on wire basket. Spray croquettes with oil. Bake in air fryer at 350 degrees F for 20 minutes. Serve warm with tartar sauce. Makes 4–6 servings.

HEAVENLY HALIBUT

4 (6-ounce)	**skinless halibut fillets**
I teaspoon each	**salt and pepper**
$^1/_2$ cup	**finely grated Parmesan cheese**
$^1/_4$ cup	**mayonnaise**
2 tablespoons	**thinly sliced green onion**
I teaspoon	**lemon-pepper seasoning**
$^1/_4$ teaspoon	**cayenne pepper**

Sprinkle halibut fillets on both sides with salt and pepper. Spray baking sheet with nonstick cooking oil. Place fillets on baking sheet and then spray with oil. Bake in air fryer at 400 degrees F for 5 minutes.

Mix together cheese, mayonnaise, green onion, lemon-pepper seasoning, and cayenne pepper. Spread cheese mixture on tops of fillets. Bake in air fryer for about 3 more minutes, until tops are bubbly and lightly browned. Serve immediately. Makes 4 servings.

GROWNUP FISH STICKS

4 (6-ounce)	**skinless cod fillets**
2 teaspoons	**salt**
2 teaspoons	**lemon-pepper seasoning**
$^1/_2$ cup	**flour**
1	**large egg,** whisked with 1 tablespoon water
1 $^1/_2$ cups	**panko-style breadcrumbs**
$^1/_2$ cup	**finely grated Parmesan cheese**
	tartar sauce, for serving

Cut cod into planks that are 1-inch thick. Sprinkle all sides of cod planks with salt and lemon-pepper seasoning. Spread flour on a shallow bowl or plate. Pour egg mixture into a separate shallow bowl. Combine the Parmesan cheese with the breadcrumbs and add to a third shallow bowl or plate.

Dip all sides of each piece of fish into flour and shake off excess. Dip fish pieces into egg mixture, coating all sides. Press fish pieces on all sides into breadcrumb mixture, pressing down so that pieces are well coated. Chill coated fish in refrigerator for 10 minutes.

Spray fish with oil on all sides and place on wire basket. Bake in air fryer at 350 degrees F for about 18–20 minutes, until fish is cooked through and golden brown.

Serve immediately with tartar sauce. Makes 4–6 servings.

OLD BAY SHRIMP, TOMATOES, AND FETA

16 ounces	**large raw shrimp,** peeled and deveined
5 cloves	**garlic,** thinly sliced
1 tablespoon	**lemon juice**
3 tablespoons	**olive oil**
1 tablespoon	**Old Bay Seasoning***
1 cup	**grape tomatoes**
4 ounces	**feta cheese,** cut in small cubes
1/4 cup	**chopped parsley**

Stir together shrimp, garlic, lemon juice, oil, and Old Bay seasoning. Let sit on countertop for 20 minutes, stirring occasionally.

Cut tomatoes in half and toss with shrimp mixture. Spread in a single layer on baking sheet, leaving space between shrimp and tomatoes. Bake in air fryer at 450 degrees F for 5 minutes. Remove from air fryer, turn mixture over with a wide spatula. Scatter feta cubes onto baking sheet with shrimp mixture. Bake for another 3 minutes.

Sprinkle parsley on top and serve immediately. Makes 4–6 servings.

*If you cannot purchase Old Bay Seasoning, mix together 1 tablespoon celery salt and 1/2 teaspoon regular or smoked paprika. Add pinches of the following: cayenne pepper, dry mustard, cinnamon, allspice, and ginger.

ASIAN-GLAZED SALMON

2 tablespoons	**hoisin sauce**
I tablespoon	**lime juice**
I teaspoon	**minced garlic**
I teaspoon	**grated ginger**
4 (6-ounce)	**skinless salmon fillets**
I teaspoon each	**salt and pepper**

Stir together the hoisin, lime juice, garlic, and ginger. Sprinkle each piece of salmon with salt and pepper on all sides. Spray wire basket with cooking oil. Place salmon on wire basket. Spread half of sauce mixture on tops of fish.

Bake in air fryer at 375 degrees F for 8 minutes. Remove from air fryer and spread all remaining sauce on tops of salmon. Bake for another 5 minutes. Turn off air fryer and let salmon sit for about 5 minutes to ensure that salmon is cooked through. Serve immediately. Makes 4 servings.

COCONUT
BANG BANG SHRIMP

16 ounces	**large shrimp,** peeled and deveined
4 cups	**cold water**
2 tablespoons	**salt**
1/2 cup	**cornstarch**
1 teaspoon	**chili powder**
1 cup	**mayonnaise,** divided
1/3 cup	**cayenne pepper sauce**
1 cup	**panko-style breadcrumbs**
1/2 cup	**minced unsweetened coconut flakes**
2 tablespoons	**sweet chili sauce**
1 tablespoon	**lime juice**

Place shrimp in water and salt and let sit for 10 minutes. Drain, rinse, and pat dry with a paper towel.

In a shallow bowl or pan, mix together the cornstarch and chili powder. In another shallow bowl or pan, mix together 2/3 cup mayonnaise and pepper sauce. In a third shallow bowl or pan, mix together breadcrumbs and coconut flakes.

Coat shrimp with cornstarch mixture, then in mayonnaise mixture, then in breadcrumb mixture. Place on wire basket that has been sprayed with cooking oil. Spray shrimp with oil. Bake in air fryer at 350 degrees F for 5 minutes. Turn shrimp over and spray again with oil. Bake for another 3–5 minutes, until golden brown.

Stir together remaining mayonnaise, sweet chili sauce, and lime juice. Drizzle on top of shrimp or serve on the side for dipping. Makes 4–6 servings.

VEGETARIAN MAIN DISHES

CAPRESE STUFFED PORTOBELLOS

4	**large portobello mushrooms***
3/4 cup	**fresh mozzarella pearls**
1 cup	**grape tomatoes**
2 tablespoons	**basil pesto**
3 tablespoons	**pine nuts**
1/2 cup	**balsamic vinegar**
2 tablespoons	**brown sugar**

Using a large spoon, scrape out gills and remove stems from mushrooms. Discard stems and gills. Place mushrooms on baking sheet, cleaned sides up. Spray both sides of cleaned mushrooms with cooking oil. Bake in air fryer at 350 degrees F for 3 minutes.

Stir together mozzarella pearls, tomatoes, and pesto. Spoon mixture into the mushroom caps. Sprinkle nuts on tops. Bake in air fryer for another 5 minutes.

While mushrooms are baking, simmer the vinegar and brown sugar in a small saucepan until reduced by half, whisking constantly.

Place mushrooms on a serving platter and drizzle with balsamic syrup. Serve immediately. Makes 4 servings.

*Mushrooms with a cup shape, rather than a flat shape, work best for this recipe.

GREEK ZUCCHINI-FETA CASSEROLE

I tablespoon	**olive oil**
$^1/_2$	**onion,** diced
2 medium (8 ounces each)	**zucchini**
I teaspoon	**dried oregano**
$^1/_2$ teaspoon each	**salt and pepper**
4	**large eggs**
$^1/_3$ cup	**flour**
I teaspoon	**baking powder**
$^1/_3$ cup	**plain Greek yogurt**
I block (6 ounces)	**feta cheese**
$^1/_4$ cup	**chopped parsley**
I teaspoon	**cayenne pepper sauce**

In a large skillet over medium-high heat, add oil and onion and saute for about 3 minutes. Cut zucchini in half lengthwise and then into $^1/_3$-inch-thick half-moon slices. Add zucchini, oregano, salt, and pepper to skillet and saute until zucchini is fork tender. Turn off heat and let cool to warm.

Whisk together eggs, flour, baking powder, and yogurt. Cut feta into small cubes. Stir feta, parsley, and pepper sauce into egg mixture, and then stir into skillet mixture. Spoon into an 8-inch pie or cake pan that has been sprayed with cooking oil.

Bake in air fryer at 300 degrees F for 20 minutes. Serve immediately. Makes 4–6 servings.

PIZZA-TOPPED FRITTATA

4	**large eggs**
$1/4$ cup	**heavy cream**
$1/2$ teaspoon each	**salt and pepper**
2 cups	**chopped spinach**
2	**green onions,** thinly sliced
$1/2$ cup	**diced tomatoes**
$1/2$ cup	**grated cheddar cheese**
$1/2$ cup	**marinara sauce**
$1/2$ cup	**grated mozzarella cheese**
2 tablespoons	**finely grated Parmesan cheese**

Whisk together eggs, cream, salt, and pepper. Stir in spinach, green onions, tomatoes, and cheddar cheese. Spray an 8-inch round cake pan with cooking oil. Pour in egg mixture. Bake in air fryer at 350 degrees F for 12 minutes.

Spread marinara sauce on top of frittata. Sprinkle mozzarella and Parmesan cheeses on top. Bake for another 3 minutes. Cut into wedges and serve immediately. Makes 4 servings.

FOUR CHEESE ZUCCHINI CAKES

2 medium (8 ounces each)	**zucchini**
1	**medium shallot,** finely diced
3 cloves	**garlic,** minced
1 tablespoon	**olive oil**
2	**large eggs**
2 tablespoons	**ricotta cheese**
$^1/_4$ cup	**grated mozzarella cheese**
$^1/_2$ cup	**finely grated Parmesan cheese**
$^1/_4$ cup	**crumbled feta cheese**
1 cup	**panko-style breadcrumbs**
	dash of cayenne pepper sauce
$^1/_2$ cup	**mayonnaise**
1 tablespoon	**Sriracha or other hot sauce**

Grate zucchini on large holes of a box grater. Place grated zucchini on a kitchen towel and then squeeze over the sink until most of liquid is removed.

Saute shallot and garlic in oil over medium heat for a few minutes, until softened.

Stir together shallot mixture, squeezed zucchini, eggs, cheeses, and breadcrumbs. Using $^1/_3$ cup measure, form into patties that are $^1/_2$ inch thick. Refrigerate for 10 minutes. Spray both sides of patties with cooking oil and place in wire basket, spaced apart. Bake in air fryer at 375 degrees F for 18 minutes, turning patties over halfway through cooking time.

Place patties on a serving platter. Mix together the mayonnaise and Sriracha sauce and drizzle over patties. Serve immediately. Makes 4 servings.

PHYLLO-TOPPED SPINACH PIE

1/2	**onion,** finely diced
1/2 teaspoon each	**salt and pepper**
2 tablespoons	**olive oil**
16 ounces	**baby spinach leaves**
1/4 cup	**chopped fresh dill**
2	**large eggs**
4 ounces	**feta cheese,** crumbled
1/2 teaspoon	**nutmeg**
8 sheets	**phyllo dough**
4 tablespoons	**butter,** melted

In a large skillet over medium-high heat, saute onion, salt, and pepper in oil until softened, about 3 minutes. Add in spinach, a handful at a time, and stir and cook until all spinach is wilted and most of liquid has evaporated. Remove from heat and stir in dill, eggs, feta, and nutmeg. Place skillet mixture into an 8-inch round pan that has been sprayed with cooking oil.

Lay out phyllo sheets, 1 at a time, on a cutting board. Brush the sheet with butter and place on top of spinach mixture in pan, allowing edges to hang over pan. Repeat this process until all sheets are on top. Fold edges in toward the center of the pan. Use a fork to prick the phyllo sheets all over the top.

Place pan on baking sheet and bake in air fryer at 300 degrees F for 18 minutes. Serve immediately. Makes 4 servings.

GENERAL TSO'S CAULIFLOWER

I	**small cauliflower**
2 tablespoons	**vegetable oil**
I tablespoon	**sesame oil**
2 cloves	**garlic,** minced
I tablespoon	**grated ginger**
$^1/_4$ cup	**soy sauce**
2 tablespoons	**rice vinegar**
$^1/_4$ cup	**gochujang or chili sauce**
2 tablespoons	**brown sugar**
I tablespoon	**cornstarch mixed with 2 tablespoons water**
	sesame seeds and thinly sliced green onions for garnish

Remove core and separate all the florets from the cauliflower. Cut the large florets in halves or quarters to make all florets roughly the same size. Toss the florets in oils and spread on wire basket. Bake in air fryer at 400 degrees F for 15 minutes.

While cauliflower is baking, stir together garlic, ginger, soy sauce, vinegar, gochujang, brown sugar, and cornstarch mixture and bring to a simmer in a small saucepan. Whisk and cook for 2–3 minutes, until thickened. Toss cooked cauliflower in sauce. Spread coated cauliflower on wire basket and bake in air fryer at 450 degrees F for 2 minutes. Spoon onto a serving plate and sprinkle with sesame seeds and green onions. Serve immediately. Makes 4 servings.

BUTTERMILK AIR-FRIED MUSHROOMS

8	**large cremini or white button mushrooms**
2 tablespoons	**olive oil**
I cup	**flour**
I tablespoon	**chili powder**
I teaspoon	**baking powder**
I teaspoon	**salt**
I cup	**buttermilk**
I tablespoon	**cayenne pepper sauce**
I cup	**panko-style breadcrumbs**
1/3 cup	**ranch dressing,** optional

With a small spoon, remove stems and scrape out gills from mushrooms. Toss cleaned mushrooms in oil. Place mushrooms in a single layer in wire basket. Bake in air fryer at 375 degrees F for 3 minutes. Place cooked mushrooms on a cutting board and gently flatten with a spatula.

Stir together flour, chili powder, baking powder, and salt in a shallow bowl. Mix buttermilk and pepper sauce in another shallow bowl. Spread breadcrumbs in third shallow bowl. Coat mushrooms with flour mixture, shaking to remove excess. Coat mushrooms in buttermilk mixture. Press mushrooms into breadcrumbs on both sides to ensure that they are evenly coated. Let sit on countertop for 10 minutes.

Spray wire basket with cooking oil. Place mushrooms in a single layer in wire basket. Spray mushrooms with oil. Bake in air fryer at 375 degrees F for 8 minutes. Serve immediately, drizzled with ranch dressing if desired. Makes 4 servings.

ZUCCHINI BURRITO BOATS

2	**medium zucchini,** each about 8 inches long
3 tablespoons	**vegetable oil,** divided
1 teaspoon	**salt,** divided
1/2	**poblano or Anaheim pepper,** diced
1/2	**yellow onion,** diced
2 teaspoons each	**cumin and chili powder**
1 can (15 ounces)	**black beans,** drained and rinsed
1/2 cup	**corn kernels**
1/2 cup	**salsa**
1 cup	**pepper jack cheese,** divided

Cut zucchini in half lengthwise. Using a small spoon, scrape out and discard zucchini flesh and seeds, leaving a 1/4-inch shell. Brush all sides of zucchini halves with 1 tablespoon of oil. Sprinkle with 1/2 teaspoon salt. Place, cut sides up, on baking sheet. Bake in air fryer at 350 degrees F for 3 minutes. Remove from air fryer and let cool.

In a medium skillet, heat remaining oil to medium-high heat. Saute pepper and onion until softened, about 2 minutes. Stir in remaining salt, cumin, and chili powder and saute another minute. Stir in beans, corn, salsa, and 1/2 cup cheese and cook for about 3 minutes, until very hot.

Spoon skillet mixture into zucchini and place on baking sheet. Spread remaining cheese on tops. Bake in air fryer at 350 degrees for 8 minutes. Serve immediately. Makes 4 servings.

TWICE-BAKED BUTTERNUT SQUASH

2 small (16 to 24 ounces each)	**butternut squash**
1 cup	**diced onion**
2 tablespoons	**olive oil**
1 tablespoon	**cumin**
1/2 tablespoon	**coriander**
1 teaspoon each	**salt and pepper**
1 teaspoon	**cayenne pepper sauce**
1 can (15 ounces)	**lentils,** drained and rinsed
1/2 cup	**finely diced walnuts,** divided
1/4 cup	**diced raisins**

Cut squash in half and scoop out seeds and strings. Spray with cooking oil and place, cut sides down, on baking sheet. Bake in air fryer at 400 degrees F for about 20 minutes, until flesh is fork tender. Remove squash and let cool to warm.

In a medium skillet, saute onion in oil until softened, about 3 minutes. Add in cumin, coriander, salt, and pepper and let cook another minute. Stir in pepper sauce, lentils, 1/4 cup walnuts, and raisins.

Using a large sturdy spoon, scoop out flesh from squash halves, leaving about 1/3 to 1/2 inch of flesh around the bottom and sides of the squash shells. Dice scooped-out flesh and stir into skillet mixture. Spoon skillet mixture into shells. Sprinkle remaining walnuts on tops of filled squash and press down lightly with spoon to embed walnuts into lentil mixture. Bake in air fryer for 5 minutes. Serve immediately. Makes 4 servings.

THAI SESAME-CRUSTED TOFU

I block (16 ounces)	**firm tofu**
1/2 cup	**flour**
I	**large egg**
4 tablespoons	**low-sodium soy sauce,** divided
2 tablespoons	**Sriracha or other hot sauce,** divided
1/3 cup	**black or regular sesame seeds**
1/3 cup	**panko-style breadcrumbs**
1/3 cup	**peanut butter**
3 tablespoons	**lime juice,** divided
2 tablespoons	**maple syrup or agave nectar**
I teaspoon	**sesame oil**
I cup	**thinly sliced cabbage**
1/2	**red bell pepper,** thinly sliced
I tablespoon	**olive oil**
1/4 cup	**diced roasted salted peanuts**

Wrap tofu in a folded kitchen towel. Place a cutting board on top and let sit for about 30 minutes to press moisture out.

Place flour in a small shallow bowl. In another bowl, mix egg, 2 tablespoons soy sauce, and I tablespoon Sriracha. In another bowl, mix sesame seeds and breadcrumbs. In a small bowl, whisk together peanut butter, 2 tablespoons lime juice, maple syrup, sesame oil, remaining soy sauce, and remaining Sriracha. Toss together cabbage, bell pepper, remaining lime juice, olive oil, and peanuts.

Slice tofu into 2-inch-thick rectangles. Dip the tofu into flour, then egg mixture, and then breadcrumb mixture. Place on wire basket and spray with cooking oil. Bake in air fryer at 375 degrees F for 10 minutes. Turn tofu over and spray with oil. Bake for another 3 minutes. Serve drizzled with peanut sauce and topped with cabbage mixture. Makes 4 servings.

AIR-FRYER
EGGPLANT PIZZAS

I	**large eggplant**
I tablespoon	**salt**
$3/4$ cup	**marinara sauce**
I cup	**favorite pizza toppings, such as sliced olives, diced onions, or peppers**
I cup	**grated mozzarella cheese**
$1/2$ cup	**grated Parmesan cheese**

Slice eggplant into 6 large slices that are $3/4$ inch thick. Generously salt both sides of slices and let sit for about 30 minutes to remove bitterness and excess moisture. Rinse off slices and pat dry.

Spray eggplant slices with cooking oil and place in wire basket. Bake in air fryer at 375 degrees F for 8 minutes. Turn slices over and bake another 3 minutes.

Remove slices and spread each with 2 tablespoons marinara sauce. Scatter each slice with pizza toppings and cheese. Bake in air fryer about another 5 minutes, until bubbly. Serve immediately. Makes 6 servings.

SWEET
TREATS

TRIPLE BERRY CRISP

4 cups	**fresh or frozen and thawed berries,** such as blackberries, blueberries, and raspberries
1/4 cup	**sugar**
1/4 cup	**orange juice**
2 tablespoons	**cornstarch**
1 cup	**yellow cake mix**
1/3 cup	**rolled oats**
1/3 cup	**chopped walnuts or pecans**
6 tablespoons	**butter,** melted
	whipped cream or vanilla ice cream for serving

Spread berries on a cutting board and smash lightly with a potato masher; place into a large bowl. Stir together sugar, orange juice, and cornstarch. Stir liquid into berries. Spoon into an 8 x 8-inch baking pan.

Stir together cake mix, oats, and nuts. Spoon this mixture evenly on top of berry mixture. Drizzle top with butter.

Bake in air fryer at 300 degrees F for 22–24 minutes, until lightly browned and bubbly. Serve with whipped cream or ice cream. Makes 4–6 servings.

PINK PEARS IN PUFF PASTRY

4 cups	**water**
1/2	**lemon,** cut in quarters
2 tablespoons	**cinnamon red hots candies***
4	**small ripe but firm Bartlett pears**
2 tablespoons	**sugar**
1 1/2 tablespoons	**cornstarch**
1 sheet	**frozen puff pastry,** thawed
1	**large egg,** whisked with 1 tablespoon water

Place water, lemon, and cinnamon candies in a medium saucepan. Bring water to a boil. Use a small paring knife to core pears from the bottom by making long cuts into the center of pears in a circular manner. Peel the pears, leaving the stem on top.

Place pears in water and simmer for 5–10 minutes, checking frequently, until fork tender. Remove pears and let cool. Strain poaching liquid and reserve 2 cups. Boil the reserved liquid to reduce by half. Mix together sugar and cornstarch and whisk into boiling liquid. Whisk and cook another 1–2 minutes, until thickened.

Gently pat pears dry with paper towels. Cut pastry into 1/2-inch-thick strips. Wrap pastry strips around pears, leaving slight gaps so that steam can escape from pears while baking. Brush with egg mixture. Bake in air fryer at 300 degrees F for 22–25 minutes, until browned. Drizzle syrup on serving plates and then set pears on top. Serve immediately. Makes 4 servings.

*If you can't find old-fashioned cinnamon red hots candies, you can use 2 cinnamon sticks. The pears won't have a lovely pink color but will still have a delicious cinnamon flavor.

SPICE CAKE IN BAKED APPLE SHELLS

4	**large Granny Smith apples**
1 box (15 ounces)	**spice cake mix**
$1/2$ cup	**apple juice**
2 tablespoons	**vegetable oil**
1	**large egg**
2 tablespoons	**cinnamon sugar**

Cut apples in half lengthwise. Scoop out and eat or discard apple flesh, leaving a $1/3$-inch shell. If needed for stability, make a small slice on bottom of apple shell so it will not wobble.

Place $1 1/2$ cups spice cake mix in a mixing bowl and reserve remainder of mix for another use. Stir in apple juice, oil, and egg. Spoon about $1/4$ cup batter into apple shells, filling to $1/2$ inch from the top of shells. Sprinkle cinnamon sugar on tops.

Place on baking sheet and bake in air fryer at 250 degrees F for 18–20 minutes, or until cake is set. Makes 8 servings.

CAMPFIRE-FREE
S'MORES DESSERT

1/2 cup	**coconut milk**
2 tablespoons	**light corn syrup**
2 (7-ounce)	**milk chocolate bars**
2 tablespoons	**coconut oil,** melted
1 package (8 ounces)	**marshmallows**
	graham crackers, for serving

In a glass bowl, heat coconut milk and corn syrup in microwave oven until very hot, about 90 seconds. Break up chocolate bars and stir into bowl, melting chocolate. If needed, microwave for additional 10 seconds at a time to make mixture smooth.

Pour oil into an 8-inch round cake pan. Pour chocolate mixture into pan. Place marshmallows on top, arranging in a circular pattern so that entire surface is covered.

Bake in air fryer at 350 degrees F for 1–2 minutes, watching closely so as not to burn tops of marshmallows. Serve immediately with graham crackers for dipping. Makes 4–6 servings.

APPLE-CINNAMON CHIPS WITH ALMOND DIP

1	**large Granny Smith apple**
1 tablespoon	**lemon juice**
1/4 cup	**sugar**
2 teaspoons	**cinnamon**
1/2 cup	**vanilla Greek yogurt**
2 tablespoons	**almond butter**
1 teaspoon	**almond extract**
2 tablespoons	**honey**

Cut apple into paper-thin round slices, cut a small circle out of center of each slice to remove seeds, and toss slices with lemon juice. Spray wire basket with cooking oil. Place apple slices in a single layer in basket. Bake in air fryer at 325 degrees F for 8–10 minutes, until just beginning to brown around edges. Watch closely the last few minutes so as not to burn chips.

Mix together sugar and cinnamon. Remove apple slices, and while still warm, sprinkle with cinnamon sugar. Let cool completely. Slices will crisp up as they cool.

Stir together yogurt, almond butter, almond extract, and honey. Use as a dip for apple chips. Makes 12 chips.

FLOURLESS BROWNIE COOKIES

1	**ripe but firm avocado**
1 cup	**cocoa powder**
2	**large eggs**
2/3 cup	**sugar**
2 tablespoons	**almond or peanut butter**
1 teaspoon	**vanilla extract**
1/4 teaspoon	**salt**
1/2 cup	**chocolate chips**
1/2 cup	**diced pecans or walnuts**

In a large bowl, mash avocado with a fork. Stir in cocoa powder, eggs, sugar, almond butter, vanilla, salt, chocolate chips, and nuts.

Scoop 2 tablespoons of cookie batter onto oiled baking sheet, leaving space between scoops and cooking in separate batches as necessary to fit on baking sheet. Dip fork into a little water and press fork on top of each cookie scoop to flatten to a cookie shape.

Bake in air fryer at 350 degrees F for 8 minutes. Let cool to warm and serve. Makes 18 cookies.

SHORTCUT APPLE CROSTATA

1	**large Gala or Golden Delicious apple**
2 tablespoons	**lemon juice**
1 tablespoon	**cornstarch**
4 tablespoons	**sugar**
1 teaspoon	**cinnamon**
	pinch of salt
4 tablespoons	**cold butter**
1	**purchased pie dough round,**
	12 inches in diameter

Turn air fryer to 350 degrees F. Place baking sheet in air fryer and let heat for about 5 minutes. Cut apples in half and remove core and stem. Slice apples in $1/4$-inch-thick slices. Toss apple slices with lemon juice. Mix the cornstarch, sugar, cinnamon, and salt in a large bowl. Cut in butter with a fork or pastry cutter until butter is in small bits. Toss apple slices with mixture.

Spread a piece of aluminum foil on countertop that is the size of the baking sheet. Place pie dough round on foil. Spread apples in center of pie dough, leaving 2 inches around edges of dough empty. Fold empty dough edges toward center, up and over top of the apple slices just a bit, leaving center with apple slices open. Place aluminum foil with apple crostata on top of heated baking sheet.

Bake in air fryer for about 15 minutes, until crust is golden brown and cooked through and apple mixture is bubbly. Makes 4–6 servings.

BERRIES AND CREAM DESSERT NACHOS

6 (8-inch)	**flour tortillas**
6 tablespoons	**sugar,** divided
2 teaspoons	**cinnamon**
4 ounces	**cream cheese,** softened
2 tablespoons	**lemon juice**
1 teaspoon	**lemon zest**
4 cups	**mixed berries,** such as blueberries, blackberries, raspberries, and diced strawberries

Cut each tortilla into 6 wedges. Mix 4 tablespoons of sugar with cinnamon in a small dish. Place tortilla wedges and cinnamon sugar mixture near the kitchen sink. With a small stream of water running, wet a tortilla wedge and then shake off excess water. Sprinkle both sides lightly with cinnamon sugar. Repeat until all wedges are coated.

Place coated wedges in wire basket in a single layer leaving a little space between wedges. Wedges will need to be baked in batches. Bake in air fryer at 400 degrees F for 2 minutes. Turn wedges over and bake another 1–2 minutes, until browned. Place wedges on a large serving platter and let cool. Wedges will crisp up as they cool. Repeat this process until all wedges are cooked.

Mix together cream cheese, remaining sugar, lemon juice, and zest. Arrange tortilla wedges on serving plates and then drizzle with cream cheese mixture. Scatter berries on top and serve. Makes 4–6 servings.

BEST-EVER CHOCOLATE CHIP COOKIES

1/2 cup	**butter**
1/2 cup	**sugar**
1/2 cup	**light brown sugar**
1	**large egg**
1 teaspoon	**vanilla extract**
1/2 teaspoon	**baking soda**
1/4 teaspoon	**salt**
1 1/2 cups	**flour**
1 cup	**semisweet chocolate chips**
1/2 cup	**chopped walnuts or pecans**

Cream together butter and sugars with a mixer on medium-high speed until light and fluffy. While mixer is running, add in the egg, vanilla, baking soda, and salt, mixing between additions. Turn off mixer and stir in flour, chocolate chips, and nuts.

Using a 2-tablespoon scoop, drop dough onto baking sheet, spacing 1 inch apart. Flatten each scoop with a spatula until 1/2 inch thick. Bake in batches as needed. Bake in air fryer at 300 degrees F for 10 minutes until lightly browned, watching last few minutes closely so as not to burn. Makes 18 cookies.

FOUR-INGREDIENT SHORTBREAD COOKIES

$^3/_4$ cup **butter,** room temperature
$^2/_3$ cup **superfine sugar,** divided, plus a little more for rolling dough
2 cups plus 2 tablespoons **flour**
$^1/_4$ cup **water**

Place butter and $^1/_2$ cup sugar in a large bowl and mix with electric mixer at medium-high speed for about 3 minutes, until light and fluffy. Slowly pour in flour with mixer at medium speed. Drizzle in up to $^1/_4$ cup water as needed just until dough begins to come together.

Dump dough out onto a sheet of waxed or parchment paper. Using paper to help form a roll, gently roll dough into a long cylinder log shape, about $2^1/_2$ inches in diameter. Wrap with paper and refrigerate for at least 20 minutes.

Cut into round slices that are between $^1/_4$ and $^1/_2$ inch thick. Place on baking sheet. Bake in air fryer at 300 degrees F for 15–18 minutes, until cooked through in center. Turn off air fryer and let sit for a few minutes, ensuring that cookies are done on bottoms. Makes 12 cookies.

APPLE PIE EGG ROLLS

3 cups	**diced, peeled apples**
1 tablespoon	**lemon juice**
1 tablespoon	**butter**
2 teaspoons	**cinnamon,** divided
1/4 cup	**powdered sugar**
1/2 cup	**apple juice**
8 (8-inch)	**eggroll wrappers**
1/4 cup	**sugar**
	whipped cream, for serving

Toss apples in lemon juice. Heat a skillet to medium-high heat. Add butter, apples, and 1 teaspoon cinnamon. Saute for a few minutes, until apples are fork tender. Stir powdered sugar into apple juice and add to skillet. Stir and cook until apples are tender and most of liquid has evaporated. Let cool to warm.

Spread an eggroll wrapper out on a flat surface. Scoop 1/4 cup of apple mixture onto wrapper in a line on the side closest to you. Wet edges of wrapper on all 4 sides. Roll up like you would a burrito, tucking in edges at sides.

Spray wire basket with cooking oil. Place eggrolls on wire basket and spray lightly with oil. Bake in air fryer 325 degrees F for 8 minutes. Turn eggrolls over, spray lightly with oil, and bake for another 4–5 minutes, until lightly browned. Mix remaining cinnamon with sugar and spread on a small plate. While eggrolls are still hot, roll in sugar mixture. Serve warm, with whipped cream if desired. Makes 4–6 servings.

FRUIT-TOPPED CHEESECAKE TART

I sheet	**frozen puff pastry,** thawed
6 ounces	**cream cheese**
I teaspoon	**lemon zest**
2 tablespoons	**lemon juice**
$1/3$ cup	**sugar**
$2/3$ cup	**heavy cream**
2 cups	**diced fruit and/or berries**

Cut puff pastry sheet into 4 (4$1/2$-inch) squares. Prick the pastry squares every $1/2$ inch with a fork. Place on baking sheet. Bake in air fryer at 300 degrees F for 10 minutes. Remove from oven and turn squares over. Gently press squares flat with a kitchen towel. Bake for another 10 minutes. Remove from oven and let cool.

While pastry is cooking, whip the cream cheese, lemon zest, lemon juice, and sugar on high speed with a mixer for about 2 minutes until creamy. Slowly pour in the cream while mixing and whip another 2 minutes or so until fluffy. Spread $1/3$ cup of mixture onto each pastry square. Refrigerate for about 20 minutes. Spoon fruit on tops and serve. Makes 4 servings.

STATE FAIR-STYLE FUNNEL CAKES

1 cup	**water**
¹/₂ cup	**unsalted butter**
¹/₄ teaspoon	**salt**
1 cup	**bread flour**
4	**large eggs**
2 tablespoons	**sour cream or plain Greek yogurt**
	powdered sugar, for garnish

Place baking sheet into air fryer to preheat at 350 degrees F. In medium saucepan over medium-high heat, bring water, butter, and salt to a boil. Add flour all at once and stir vigorously and cook for another 1–2 minutes, until the mixture forms a ball. Remove from heat and let cool to warm.

Add in eggs, 1 at a time, stirring until well incorporated. Stir in sour cream. Scoop mixture into a large pastry bag or zip top bag with the bottom corner cut off to make a hole that is between ¹/₄ and ¹/₂ inch wide.

Spray cooking oil onto baking sheet. Pipe batter onto baking sheet in a random squiggles, forming a circle in middle of baking sheet. Spray top with oil. Bake in air fryer for 8–10 minutes, until dough is browned and cooked through. Repeat with remaining dough.

Place on a serving plate and dust with powdered sugar. Serve immediately. Makes 2 funnel cakes.

SUMMER FRUIT SHORTCAKES

I cup	**flour**
1/3 cup	**sugar**
2 teaspoons	**baking powder**
1/4 teaspoon	**salt**
I tablespoon	**minced crystallized ginger,** optional
1/3 cup	**milk**
I	**large egg**
I teaspoon	**vanilla extract**
2 tablespoons	**butter,** melted
2 cups	**diced summer fruit or berries,** either plain or with a little sugar stirred in
2 cups	**sweetened whipped cream**

Whisk together flour, sugar, baking powder, salt, and ginger, if using. In a separate small bowl, whisk milk, egg, and vanilla together and then stir liquid into dry ingredients. Pat dough out on a cutting board to a 2-inch thickness. Cut dough into 6 squares. Spray baking sheet with cooking oil. Place shortcakes on baking sheet. Bake in air fryer at 325 degrees F for 10 minutes.

Remove shortcakes from air fryer and cut in half through middles. Place on serving plates cut sides up and let cool for a few minutes to let steam escape from shortcakes. Spoon fruit and whipped cream on tops and serve. Makes 6 servings.

AIR-FRYER BANANA BOATS

4	**large, ripe but firm bananas**
1 tablespoon	**butter,** melted
$^1/_4$ cup	**milk chocolate chips,** divided
$^1/_4$ cup	**butterscotch chips,** divided
1 cup	**mini marshmallows,** divided
4	**graham crackers,** crumbled

Leaving peels on, cut bananas almost in half lengthwise, leaving bottom edge attached. Open bananas like a book and place on wire basket. Bananas should be crowded together to make sure that they remain in a "v" shape during cooking. Brush banana flesh with butter. Bake in air fryer at 350 degrees F for 3 minutes.

Scatter on top of bananas with 1 tablespoon of each kind of chips. Place marshmallows on tops, pressing down slightly to adhere to chips. Bake in air fryer for about another 3 minutes, watching closely so as not to burn marshmallows. Sprinkle tops with graham cracker crumbs and serve immediately. Makes 4 banana boats.

NOTES

NOTES

METRIC CONVERSION CHART

Volume Measurements		Weight Measurements		Temperature Conversion	
U.S.	Metric	U.S.	Metric	Fahrenheit	Celsius
1 teaspoon	5 ml	1/2 ounce	15 g	250	120
1 tablespoon	15 ml	1 ounce	30 g	300	150
1/4 cup	60 ml	3 ounces	90 g	325	160
1/3 cup	75 ml	4 ounces	115 g	350	180
1/2 cup	125 ml	8 ounces	225 g	375	190
2/3 cup	150 ml	12 ounces	350 g	400	200
3/4 cup	175 ml	1 pound	450 g	425	220
1 cup	250 ml	2 1/4 pounds	1 kg	450	230

Yum! Check out these "101" favorites
for more tasty recipes:

Bacon	**More Bacon**
Beans	**More Ramen**
Beer	**More Slow Cooker**
Bundt® Pan	**Pumpkin**
Cake Mix	**Ramen Noodles**
Canned Biscuits	**Rice**
Casserole	**Sheet Pan**
Chile Peppers	**Slow Cooker**
Dutch Oven	**Toaster Oven**
Grits	**Tortilla**
Instant Pot®	**Tots**
Jar	

Each 128 pages, $9.99

Available at bookstores or directly from GIBBS SMITH
1.800.835.4993
www.gibbs-smith.com

ABOUT THE AUTHOR

Donna Kelly, a food fanatic and recipe developer, is the author of several cookbooks including *French Toast, Quesadillas, 101 Things to Do with a Tortilla,* and *101 Things to Do with An Instant Pot®.* She lives in Salt Lake City, Utah.